Computers, interfaces and communication networks

Serge Collin

Translated from the original French by
John C. C. Nelson
Department of Electrical and Electronic Engineering,
University of Leeds

Prentice Hall/Masson

First published in French by Masson, Paris, under the title
Ordinateurs, interfaces et réseaux de communication
by Serge Collin

© Masson, Paris, 1988

This edition first published in English by
Prentice Hall International and Masson

© Prentice Hall International (UK) Ltd and Masson, Paris, 1990

Typeset in 10/13pt Times by
DMD Ltd, Oxford

Printed and bound in Great Britain by
BPCC Wheatons Ltd, Exeter

Library of Congress Cataloging-in-Publication Data
are available from the publisher.

British Library Cataloguing in Publication Data

Collin, Serge *1957-*
    Computers, interfaces and communication networks.
    1. Computer systems. Communication networks
    I. Title   II. Ordinateurs, interfaces et réseaux. *English*
    I. Title
    004.6

    ISBN 0-13-163073-3

---

1 2 3 4 5 94 93 92 91 90

ISBN 0-13-163073-3

Contents

Introduction

At the present time, data transmission networks are of ever-increasing importance and this phenomenon must become more pronounced in the future. At the time of their origin, data processing techniques were confined to computing centers where the user had to be present in order to carry out the work, or send the information to be processed. Recent years have seen a decentralization of data processing, described as distributed processing, accompanied by an explosive growth in the use of minicomputers, microcomputers and 'personal computers'. At the same time, more and more powerful machines have been developed whose operation makes use of the techniques of 'pipelining' and 'parallelism'. These are intended primarily for high-speed processing of large volumes of data, in vector or matrix form, for example. Computers of this type prove to be indispensable for applications such as real-time image processing, the solution of large mathematical models containing a large number of variables, and so on.

Communication networks enable the user not only to exchange data with others and to consult databases or databanks but also, if necessary, to make use of more powerful processors than his own and specialized processors, or other data processing equipment, connected to the network. Another important advantage arises from a reduction in the risk of interruption of a data processing service if common use of similar equipment has been anticipated (for example, several printers, several processors, and so on).

It could be imagined that this process would lead directly to the disappearance of computing centers in the immediate vicinity of the user. This will not be so in the near future; there are applications for which the volume of data to be transferred is such that the existing technology of physical devices on the network does not provide sufficient transmission capacity to realize the transfer within a reasonable time. For example, the length of files that can be transmitted through the network may be limited in this way. The high-performance computers mentioned previously will, therefore, be located at computer centers of this kind.

In this work, several physical devices that are used in networks will be examined, together with the various protocols that manage the communication mechanisms. Very short distance parallel connections between computers and peripherals will also be discussed.

Chapter 1

The physical structure of networks

1.1 Types of link

Connections can be made in many different ways, such as telephone lines, optical fibers, electromagnetic waves, satellite links, and so on. Telephone lines can be divided into two categories: switched lines and leased lines. The first of these categories forms the switched telephone network; there is no permanent connection between the caller and the destination. The first step consists of establishing a connection with the correspondent. This operation is carried out every day in telephoning a subscriber to whom one wishes to speak. These switched lines clearly cannot be used when large transfers of information must be made, particularly since the transmission rate is normally limited to 4,800 baud. The second category, that of leased lines, consists of permanent lines between users. The stage of establishing the connection, which precedes communication in the previous case, does not exist here. In comparison with switched lines, leased lines allow higher transmission speeds. They are divided into two categories according to their quality:

- Normal quality, two- or four-wire, generally adequate for transmission speeds not exceeding 2,400 baud.
- Superior quality, four-wire, desirable for speeds of 4,800 baud and above.

Two-wire lines suffer from an echo problem due to spurious reflection of waves from the receiver to the transmitter. To remedy this effect, it is necessary to make provision for the suppression of echoes. The problem with a bidirectional link arises from the fact that components introduce interference and switching transients. The latter last for around 150 ms and can also be troublesome. Recall that, as soon as repeaters are required to amplify the signals on the line, as is the case for medium-and long-distance communication, the use of four-wire links becomes obligatory since these devices operate only in one direction.

1.2 Network topologies

1.2.1 Point-to-point connections

A unique communication channel can be established between two data processing systems; this is a point-to-point connection (see Figure 1.1). If there are more than two systems, a star structure can be created (see Figure 1.2). A tree structure could equally be realized, which can be regarded as a mixture of the two previous ones (see Figure 1.3).

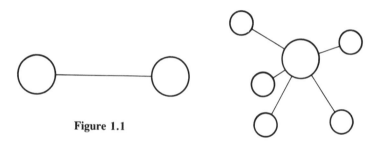

Figure 1.1

Figure 1.2

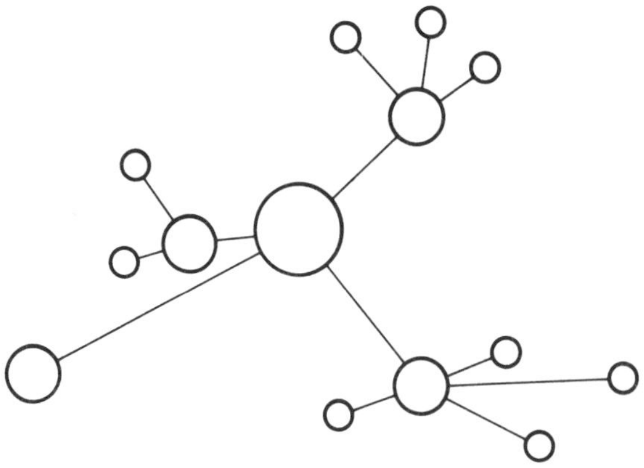

Figure 1.3

1.2.2 Multipoint connections

A multipoint connection is formed by connecting point-to-point links in series (see Figure 1.4). Figure 1.4 illustrates the case of an open link but it is also possible to close it (see Figure 1.5). In this way a loop or ring structure is created that increases the reliability of the network.

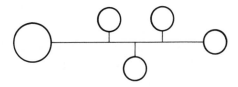

Figure 1.4

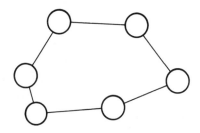

Figure 1.5

This type of network is used, for example, by IBM for their local area network, the IBM Token Ring Network. It provides high-speed communication between processing units in a local area (within a company, on a campus and so on). Finally, there is the mesh network, formed by superposition of a number of loops (see Figure 1.6).

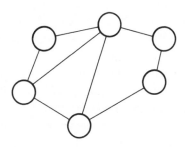

Figure 1.6

1.3 Hierarchy within a network

This concept arises naturally in telephone networks from the fact that local links are more numerous than regional ones, which in turn are more frequent than those between regions or countries. Consequently, centers are set up at each level in which the connections linking subscribers with other centers are adapted according to their function (see Figure 1.7).

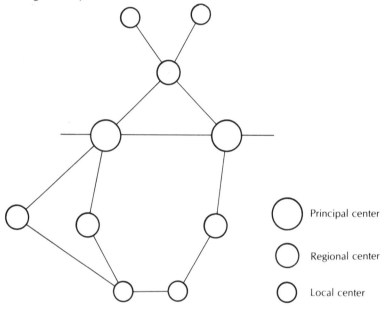

Principal center

Regional center

Local center

Figure 1.7

The same principles have been retained for data transmission networks (see Figure 1.8), except that it is not telephones that are connected together but data processing equipment or networks consisting of such equipment.

In this case, the situation is a little more complex because one is not dealing with a unique network; as shown in Figure 1.8, for example, interconnection between several local networks has been established. If the networks to be connected use different protocols, a compatibility problem must be resolved. Prediction of the performance of a hierarchical network proves to be extremely difficult even when using simulation techniques. Notice, however, that an advanced study of a network consisting of five local networks, nine ordinary nodes and a principal node has been undertaken by Logica under a contract with the National Physical Laboratory.

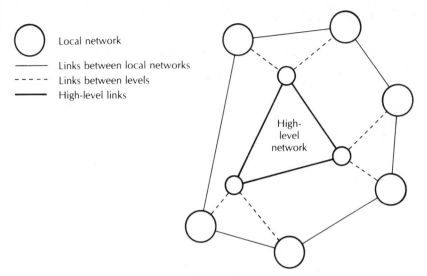

Figure 1.8

1.4 Types of link

The bits representing the coded information and any required control signals can be transmitted either sequentially, in a sequence one after the other (serial link), or grouped into words, the bits of a word being transmitted simultaneously and the words sequentially (parallel link).

1.4.1. Parallel links

As a succession of words formed from several bits must be transmitted, the structure used will be composed of as many wires as there are bits to be sent. These wires are brought together in the form of a 'bus' (see Figure 1.9). Use of such a configuration for transmission other than over a short distance is inappropriate in practice; recourse must be made to serial links. Parallel links will be dealt with later.

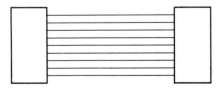

Figure 1.9

1.4.2. Serial links

When transmission is not between neighboring equipment, it is necessary, for economic reasons, to make use of serial links in which all the digital information (data signals and control signals) is transmitted in the form of sequential bits.

1.5 Transmission modes

1.5.1 Simplex connections

In this case, use is made of a unidirectional link (see Figure 1.10). There is one transmitter and one receiver and the latter cannot transmit signals in any way. Two wires are sufficient for a practical realization of a line.

Figure 1.10

1.5.2 Half duplex connections

Here, the link is bidirectional, but each of the two units can transmit only in its turn (see Figure 1.11). These links can be realized, for example, by means of a two- or four-wire connection. In the first case, it will evidently be necessary to provide echo suppressors as mentioned previously.

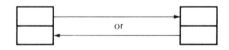

Figure 1.11

1.5.3 Full duplex connections

In this situation, the link is not only bidirectional but the two units may also transmit and receive simultaneously (see Figure 1.12). In most cases of serial transmission by telephone line, these links use four-wire lines. Use of two-wire connections is possible by means of a more sophisticated installation. In the latter case, a new echo problem arises.

Figure 1.12

To counter it, echo suppressors are again used; the process is now called echo 'cancelling' because the principle of operation is based on injection of a signal in opposition to the expected echo.

1.5.4 Asynchronous mode

In this transmission mode, the interval between two successive characters (a sequence of several bits whose number depends on the code used) is arbitrary. Consequently, signals consisting of one or more bits that mark the start and end of each character will be needed. The start signal has the effect of starting a clock at the receiver, which samples the line signal at a frequency determined by the transmission speed. The stop signal causes the receiver to return to a state such that it can detect a new character. The necessity for these signals unfortunately does not allow the full capacity of the line to be used for transmission of useful information (data). The following mode remedies this disadvantage.

1.5.5 Synchronous mode

In this transmission mode, a unique clock signal at the transmitter times the transmission of information and, at the receiver, indicates the instants when the latter must inspect the state of the line. In the case where the transmitter and receiver are in close proximity to each other, the clock can be common and its signal can be transmitted by a separate wire. In the absence of such a configuration, the clock information must be included in the transmitted data in addition to the synchronizing characters that will appear at the head of actual messages. Sometimes these signals are sent continuously in the absence of data to be transmitted. As character start and stop signals are not required, this mode of transmission proves to be more efficient than the previous one.

1.5.6 Isochronous mode

This mode consists of a compromise between the two previous ones; each character is accompanied by start and stop signals, the transmitter and receiver are synchronized but the interval between two successive characters is an exact multiple of the duration of one bit.

Chapter 2

Coding of information

2.1 General comments

The world of data processing is based essentially on the processing of information digitized in a binary form (a binary digit or bit can have a value of 0 or 1); it is, therefore, necessary to transmit binary signals.

It is necessary to establish a relationship between the character (possibly for control purposes) which it is required to transmit and its digital form as a sequence of bits; that is the code. It is evident that the greater the number of different characters to be coded, the greater the number of bits necessary to cover all possibilities.

The first person to invent a code of constant length was the Frenchman Émile Baudot in 1874. This code, which carries his name, is formed of 5 bits, which allows 32 possible codes. A clever technique has been used subsequently to increase the number of combinations while retaining the 5 bits. This code is used primarily for telegraphy.

In data processing, a widely used code is the ASCII code (American Standard Code for Information Interchange), which uses 7 bits and consequently allows 128 possibilities (see Figure 2.1 and Table 2.1). This code is defined by the American National Standard Institution and by the American version of CCITT (International Telegraph and Telephone Consultative Committee) Standard Number 5. In practice, an eighth bit is added, which permits detection of possible transmission errors. Recall that a group of 8 bits forms a 'byte'.

For completeness, mention should also be made of IBM's EBCDIC code, another currently used code.

2.2 Error detecting and correcting codes

2.2.1 The parity bit

By definition, a word is said to be even when the number of 1 bits that it contains is even; in the opposite case, the word is said to be odd.

Bits in positions 5, 6 and 7

000	100	010	110	001	101	011	111		
0	1	2	3	4	5	6	7		
NUL	DLE	SP	0	@	P	`	p	0	0000
SOH	DC1	!	1	A	Q	a	q	1	1000
STX	DC2	~	2	B	R	b	r	2	0100
ETX	DC3	#	3	C	S	c	s	3	1100
EOT	DC4	$	4	D	T	d	t	4	0010
ENQ	NAK	%	5	E	U	e	u	5	1010
ACK	SYN	&	6	F	V	f	v	6	0110
BEL	ETB	'	7	G	W	g	w	7	1110
BS	CAN	(	8	H	X	h	x	8	0001
HT	EM	)	9	I	Y	i	y	9	1001
LF	SUB	°	:	J	Z	j	z	10	0101
VT	ESC	+	;	K	[	k	{	11	1101
FF	FS	,	<	L	\	l	!	12	0011
CR	GS	–	=	M	]	m	}	13	1011
SO	RS	.	>	N	^	n	~	14	0111
SI	US	/	?	O	-	o	DEL	15	1111

Bits in positions 1, 2, 3 and 4

Figure 2.1

For example, as has previously been noted, the addition of an eighth bit to the 7 bits of the ASCII code to make it even or odd allows the detection of errors but not their correction; if words must be even, reception of an odd word signifies that it is erroneous and a repeat transmission must be recuested. Notice, however, that an even number of errors unfortunately cannot be detected. The type of parity to which reference is made here is called transverse parity. To remedy the shortcoming mentioned earlier when messages are sent in blocks of several tens of characters, a control character is added to the block; this is called longitudinal parity. Figure 2.2 illustrates generation of odd parity as used for verification of the accuracy of the received message.

Table 2.1

SP	Space
DEL	Delete
NUL	Absence of character
SOH	Start of Header
STX	Start of Text (end of header)
ETX	End of Text, started with STX
EOT	End of Transmission
ENQ	Enquiry: can be used to request the destination to identify itself
ACK	Acknowledge reception
BEL	Bell
BS	Backspace by 1 character
HT	Horizontal Tabulation
VT	Vertical Tabulation
FF	Form Feed: move to the following page
CR	Carriage Return
SO	Shift Out: the following code is outside the standard character set; terminates with 'Shift In'
SI	Shift In: return to standard characters of the code used
DC1, DC2, DC3, DC4	Device Controls . . .: control characters for terminals or peripherals
DLE	Data Link Escape: change the significance of one or more following characters
NAK	Negative Acknowledgment: negative response to a question
SYN	Synchronous/Idle: synchronization character; when no character is transmitted it can be sent continuously
ETB	End of Transmission Block: end of transmission of a block of data
CAN	Cancel: cancellation of the preceding data
EM	End of Medium: physical end of the card, tape or other medium used
SUB	Substitute
ESC	Escape: control character permitting extension of coded facilities
FS, GS, RS, US	File, Group, Record, United Separator: optional hierarchical separation characters

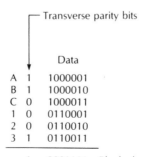

```
                    ┌─ Transverse parity bits
                    │

                    │      Data
                    ▼
            A   1   1000001
            B   1   1000010
            C   0   1000011
            1   0   0110001
            2   0   0110010
            3   1   0110011

            1   0001111   Block check characters
```

Figure 2.2

2.2.2 Hamming codes

Hamming codes are fundamentally simple error detection and correction codes. A certain number of parity bits, each one associated with a specified group of data bits, is assigned to the data word. Consider, for example, how this applies in the case of a 4-bit code such as the hexadecimal code (Table 2.2).

Let the code be written in columns 3, 5, 6 and 7 of a 7-bit word, numbered 1–7 from left to right. A bit such that the number of 'ones' in columns 4, 5, 6 and 7 is even is placed in column 4. The operation is repeated for columns 2, 3, 6 and 7 and for 1, 3, 5 and 7. Table 2.3 is obtained.

Table 2.2   **Table 2.3**

Hex	Binary	Hex	1	2	3	4	5	6	7
0	0000	0	0	0	0	0	0	0	0
1	0001	1	1	1	0	1	0	0	1
2	0010	2	0	1	0	1	0	1	0
3	0011	3	1	0	0	0	0	1	1
4	0100	4	1	0	0	1	1	0	0
5	0101	5	0	1	0	0	1	0	1
6	0110	6	1	1	0	0	1	1	0
7	0111	7	0	0	0	1	1	1	1
8	1000	8	1	1	1	0	0	0	0
9	1001	9	0	0	1	1	0	0	1
A	1010	A	1	0	1	1	0	1	0
B	1011	B	0	1	1	0	0	1	1
C	1100	C	0	1	1	1	1	0	0
D	1101	D	1	0	1	0	1	0	1
E	1110	E	0	0	1	0	1	1	0
F	1111	F	1	1	1	1	1	1	1

Assume that code C is sent, that is 0111100, and that 0111101 is obtained at the receiver. At the receiver the data are subjected to the three checking steps shown in Figure 2.3.

The binary number formed by (3)(2)(1), called the 'syndrome' word gives the number of the column where the error occurs, 7 in the present case. To make a correction, the corresponding bit in this column must be complemented; the character C is correctly recovered.

	1	2	3	4	5	6	7	
1,3,5,7	0		1		1		1	Error 1 (1)
2,3,6,7		1	1			0	1	Error 1 (2)
4,5,6,7				1	1	0	1	Error 1 (3)

Figure 2.3

On first sight it seems that, in this method, the number of check bits increases in proportion to that of the data bits, 3 check bits for 4 data bits in the preceding example. In fact, this is not so since the number of check bits (p) is related to that of the data bits (d) by an approximately logarithmic law:

$$p \simeq \log_2 (d)$$

It follows that the increase in the necessary number of check bits is much less than that of the useful bits; hence for 26 data bits, 5 check bits are sufficient.

2.2.3 Cyclic redundancy check codes (CRC)

In order to approach 100 percent error detection, other codes have been proposed; the most common are cyclic redundancy check codes (CRC) where the message is represented in the form of a polynomial:

$$P(x) = a_n x^n + a_{n-1} x^{n-1} + \ldots + a_1 x^1 + a_0 x^0$$

where the coefficients a_i can take only the value 0 or 1 and x takes the value 2.

The checking code to be associated with the data bits will consist of the remainder of the division of the polynomial $P(x)$ by a generating polynomial $G(x)$; various examples of generating polynomials are given in Table 2.4. CRC-CCITT is the European standard for messages of 8 or 16 bits; above 12 bits its reliability is of the order of 99 percent. CRC-16 is an American standard giving a reliability of 99 percent above 16 bits.

Table 2.4

Name	Polynomial
LRCC-8	x^8+1
LRCC-16	$x^{16}+1$
CRC 12	$x^{12}+x^{11}+x^3+x^2+x+1$
CRC 16 forward	$x^{16}+x^{15}+x^2+1$
CRC 16 backward	$x^{16}+x^{14}+x+1$
CRC-CCITT forward	$x^{16}+x^{12}+x^5+1$
CRC-CCITT backward	$x^{16}+x^{11}+x^4+1$

A polynomial is called 'backward' when it is possible to operate in reverse and perform a second calculation of the CRC; this can prove useful when using magnetic tapes.

At the receiver, the group of data and check bits is again divided by $G(x)$. If the remainder is not zero, an error has occurred in the transmission, otherwise two situations are possible: either the received message is correct or the erroneous polynomial $E(x)$ is itself divisible by $G(x)$ and the error consequently remains undetected. It is, therefore, necessary that the polynomial $G(x)$ should be sufficiently elaborate for such cases to occur very rarely. If the error affects a single bit, correction by trial and error can be considered where each bit is modified in turn. In principle, only modification of the erroneous bit will cause elimination of the remainder since, in other cases, a double error will occur and will be detected. For multiple errors, implementation of a similar procedure rapidly proves to be excessive in practice.

For the present, consider how the operation performs by assuming that the message to be transmitted is formed of the 4 bits, 1000 and the generating polynomial is $G(x) = x^2 + 1$.

The divisions are performed according to the following rules:

- A number of zeros equal to the number of bits in the divisor less 1 (two zeros in this case) is added to the right of the dividend.
- The division is performed by successive subtractions in modulo 2 arithmetic.

The check bits will first be determined:

```
  1000 00
 −101
 ───────
    10 0
  −10 1
  ──────
     10
```

1000 10 will therefore be transmitted.

Assume that 1000 10 is obtained at the receiver; checking gives:

```
  1000 10
 −101
 ───────
    10 1
  −10 1
  ──────
     00
```

Since the received message is correct, it is appropriate that a zero remainder is obtained. Now assume that 1001 10 is obtained instead of 1000 10; checking will lead to:

```
  1001 10
 −101
 ───────
    11 1
  −10 1
  ──────
     1 00
   −1 01
   ──────
      01
```

The remainder is not zero because an error has occurred. In contrast, if 1101 10 had occurred in place of 1000 10, the error would not have been detected as can be seen:

$$
\begin{array}{r}
1101\ 10 \\
-\,101\ \quad \\
\hline
111\ \quad \\
-\,101\ \quad \\
\hline
10\ 1 \\
-\,10\ 1 \\
\hline
00
\end{array}
$$

In this last example, the erroneous polynomial is divisible by $G(x)$, which avoids detection as already noted.

Implementation of check bit generation and received message checking is achieved not by programming but by the use of shift registers divided into sections by exclusive OR (XOR) gates; these gates consist effectively of modulo 2 adders or subtractors. The separation depends on the structure and the standard used; there are as many cells as there are check bits. Figure 2.4 gives an example for the case of messages containing a 5-bit CRC. Initially, all cells are initialized to zero. After $k + n + 1$ shifts to the right, where n is the degree of $P(x)$, k is that of $G(x)$ and, starting with the most significant bit, the register will contain the remainder with its highest weighted bit in the extreme right position.

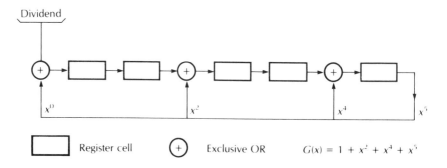

Figure 2.4

2.3 Automatic request for repeat (ARQ)

When an error is detected, it is necessary to correct it; this can be achieved by requesting a repetition, for example. Various procedures are possible.

After each transmission of a block of information, the transmitter waits for an acknowledgment of reception before sending further data. A positive acknowledgment (ACK) is transmitted if there is no error and this authorizes transmission of the following block. Retransmission occurs either automatically if acknowledgment is not received within a certain time or by sending a negative acknowledgment (NAK) which indicates an error.

In the case of a very long transmission line or a line of very wide bandwidth, this method is not well suited since the line will only be used for a small fraction of the time, the larger part being spent waiting for reception acknowledgments. Consequently, it is preferable to allow transmission of a number of blocks of information ('window width') before receiving reception acknowledgments. It is, therefore, necessary to be able to identify each block, for example by a sequence number. In the case of an error, the whole message starting from the erroneous block, or only the block itself, may be retransmitted.

Chapter 3

Parallel links

3.1 General comments

These arise from the fact that digital information is coded in the form of several bits grouped in words of 4, 8, 16 or even 32 bits. In order to obtain increased execution speeds, it is desirable to be able to transfer information in parallel; the bits of a word are sent simultaneously over several conductors, each of which corresponds to one bit. There will therefore be as many conductors as there are bits in the word. The set of conductors is called a 'bus'.

Various configurations can be adopted. There can be a single bus (see Figure 3.1) that serves the internal and external systems; the risk of saturation is increased if many elements are connected to it.

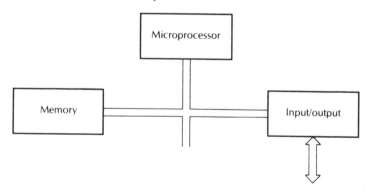

Figure 3.1

It is often possible to divide this single bus into three separate buses (see Figure 3.2) as follows:

- The data bus, which is bidirectional and consists of as many wires as there are bits in the data word.

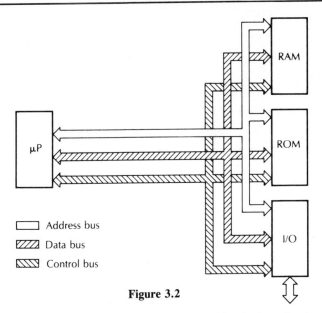

Figure 3.2

- The address bus, which is unidirectional and feeds the selection signals to input/output devices, memory cells and various interfaces.
- The control bus, which carries the control signals (clock, read/write, interrupts, and so on).

Another structure consists of a double bus with separation of function:

- A memory and an input/output bus (see Figure 3.3).
- Internal and external buses (see Figure 3.4).

A triple-bus solution can also be found, as used by Intel – an internal bus, a RAM access bus and an external bus (see Figure 3.5).

It should also be noted that, at the present time, multiple-processor systems are being developed with the processors situated at the vertices of n-dimensional hypercubes (see Figure 3.6). Using this procedure, the internal bus, whose bandwidth limits the number of processors that can be connected, is eliminated. Each processor can communicate with its neighbors. An architecture of this kind is useful in multiprocessor machines in which processing of information is carried out with a degree of parallelism, unlike sequential computers operating according to von Neumann's principle; the speed of execution is increased considerably. Unfortunately, if much communication occurs between processors, there is a certain loss of efficiency.

The bus structure, initially internal to the machine, has been extended to input/output connections with the external world for links not exceeding a few meters.

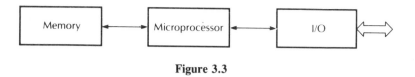

Figure 3.3

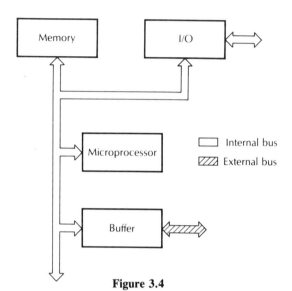

Figure 3.4

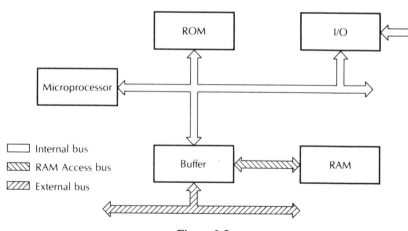

Figure 3.5

Three types of parallel interface will be reviewed:

- General-purpose input/output interfaces.
- The Centronics interface for connection to printers.
- The IEEE-488 interface for interconnection of measuring equipment.

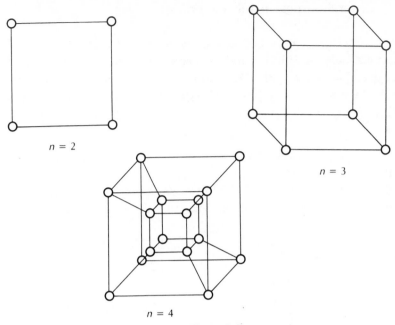

Figure 3.6

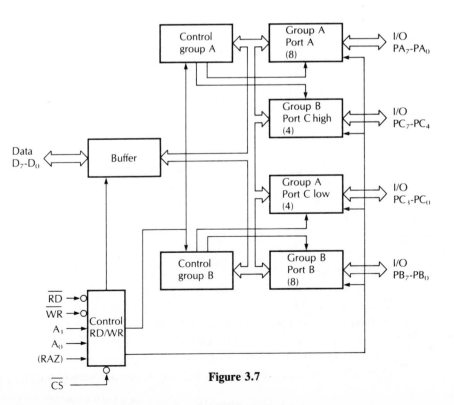

Figure 3.7

3.2 General-purpose parallel interfaces

These interfaces consist of devices with various names: peripheral interface adaptor (PIA), parallel input/output (PIO), programmable peripheral interface (PPI). Figure 3.7 shows the internal block diagram of the Intel 8255 PIA and Figure 3.8 gives the pin-out. Examination of Figure 3.7 shows that there are three programmable 8-bit input/output ports:

- Port A, which belongs to group A.
- Port B, which belongs to group B.
- Port C, which is sub-divided into two parts, the four high-order bits belong to group A and the four low-order bits to group B.

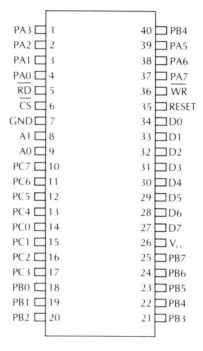

Figure 3.8

These two groups are controlled by the control circuits of each of groups A and B. Notice the presence of a bidirectional 8-bit data bus (D0–D7), pins for device selection (Chip Select), writing (WRite), reading (ReaD), reset, port and control register addressing (A0 and A1). Access to the various registers is obtained as shown in Table 3.1. The Intel 8255 has three modes of operation as represented in Figure 3.9. The control register itself has two configurations according to the

Table 3.1

Pin A0	A1	$\overline{RD}$	$\overline{WR}$	$\overline{CS}$	Operation
0	0	0	1	0	Read from port A
0	1	0	1	0	Read from port B
1	0	0	1	0	Read from port C
0	0	1	0	0	Write to port A
0	1	1	0	0	Write to port B
1	0	1	0	0	Write to port C
1	1	1	0	0	Write to control register
X	X	X	X	1	No operation
1	1	0	1	0	Illegal
X	X	1	1	0	No operation

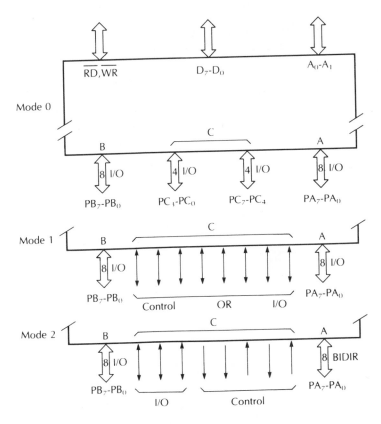

Figure 3.9

value of the highest-order bit that it contains, as shown in Figures 3.10
and 3.11. When bit D7 is at 0 it is possible to set the bit of port C
selected by means of D3, D2 and D1 to the same value as bit D0. The
different modes of operation will now be reviewed.

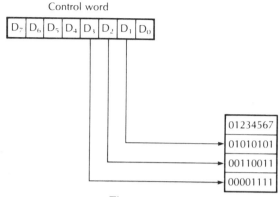

Figure 3.10

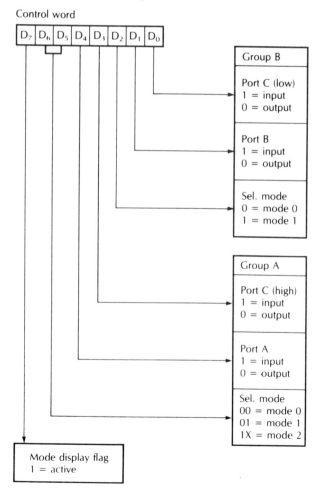

Figure 3.11

Mode 0   This is the basic input/output mode, without control; the inputs are not stored but the outputs are (data buffer).

Mode 1   This is the sampled input/output mode; port C is reserved for status and sampling control signals. Figures 3.12 and 3.13 give the timing diagrams in mode 1 for input and output, respectively.

Mode 2   Port A provides bidirectional access controlled by five lines of port C while port B can operate in mode 0 or 1, the remaining bits of port C serve as input/outputs or for control of port B. Figure 3.14 gives the timing diagram for port A.

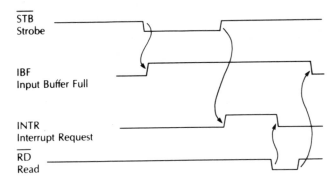

STB
Strobe

IBF
Input Buffer Full

INTR
Interrupt Request

$\overline{RD}$
Read

Figure 3.12

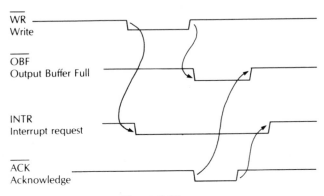

$\overline{WR}$
Write

$\overline{OBF}$
Output Buffer Full

INTR
Interrupt request

$\overline{ACK}$
Acknowledge

Figure 3.13

Figures 3.15 and 3.16 represent the internal block diagram of the Motorola 6821 PIA and its connection to a Motorola 6800 microprocessor, respectively. The reader will notice immediately that the structure of this PIA is extremely similar to that previously studied; this is the reason why no further explanation will be given.

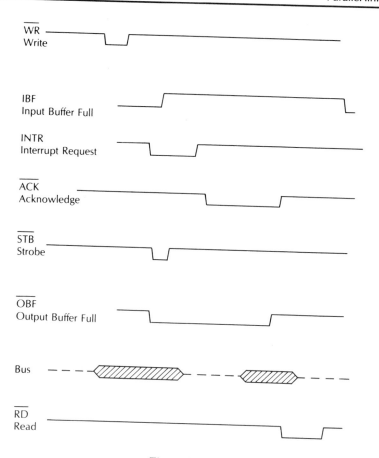

Figure 3.14

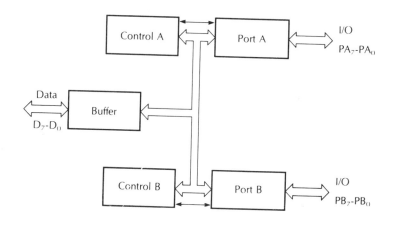

Figure 3.15

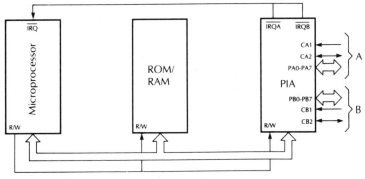

Figure 3.16

3.3 The Centronics interface

This parallel connection with a printer uses relatively low logic levels of 0 and 5 V. It follows that the distance between two units connected in this way cannot be very great, a typical value is of the order of 1–2 meters. For greater distances, it is better to use a serial link; this choice is also appropriate for economic reasons. Table 3.2 lists the various signals used.

The basic elements of the interface consist of eight data lines and three control lines – STROBE, which comes from the computer and indicates that the data present on the bus is valid, ACKnowledge and BUSY. The presence of other signals in Table 3.2 depends on the hardware used.

Table 3.2

Pin	Signal name	Pin	Signal name
1	STROBE	19	OV (return of 1)
2	DATA1	20	OV (return of 2)
3	DATA2	21	OV (return of 3)
4	DATA3	22	OV (return of 4)
5	DATA4	23	OV (return of 5)
6	DATA5	24	OV (return of 6)
7	DATA6	25	OV (return of 7)
8	DATA7	26	OV (return of 8)
9	DATA 8	27	OV (return of 9)
10	ACK	28	OV (return of 10)
11	BUSY	29	OV (return of 11)
12	PE (Paper out)	30	OV
13	BUSY	31	NC (not connected)
14	NC (not connected)	32	FAULT (error indication)
15	NC (not connected)	33	INIT (not connected)
16	OV	34	NC (not connected)
17	GROUND	35	NC (not connected)
18	NC (not connected)	36	NC (not connected)

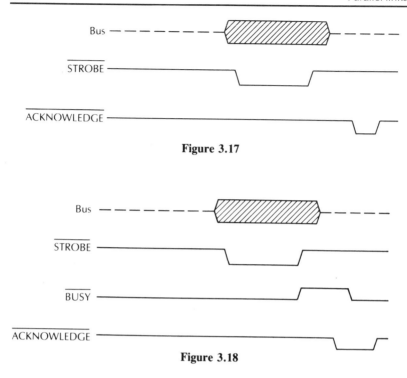

Figure 3.17

Figure 3.18

The timing diagrams are represented in Figures 3.17 and 3.18 for a normal situation and for the case where the printer is not free to accept data (generation of the BUSY signal), respectively. The latter possibility can arise when the printer receives a command to print the contents of its buffer memory following a carriage return to a vertical tabulation character (a jump of one or more lines or pages, selection or deselection, and so on).

3.4 The IEEE-488 interface

The standards governing this interface have been drawn up by the Institute of Electrical and Electronics Engineers, hence its name; it is also called the GPIB (General Purpose Interface Bus) interface. Its purpose is to allow interconnection of a computer, programmable measuring instruments and possibly plotters.

Certain restrictions should be noted:

- The maximum number of interconnected units is 15.
- More than half must be in operation.

- The maximum distance between any two units cannot exceed 4 meters.
- The total length of interconnecting cable cannot exceed 20 meters with a maximum length between two consecutive units of 2 meters.
- The speed of transfer depends on the configuration but can never be greater than 1 MB s^{-1} and is inevitably limited by the speed of transfer of the slowest unit.
- The contents of exchanged messages are not standardized.

The IEEE-488 standard ensures mechanical and electrical compatibility as well as synchronization. Figures 3.19 and 3.20 show the various

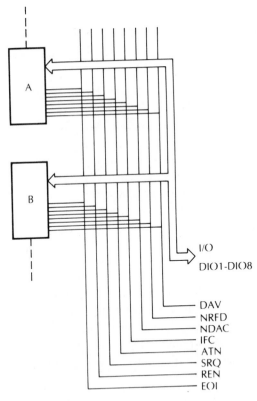

Figure 3.19

signals used and the pin-out of the connector. Negative logic is used and the signals are TTL compatible; the 0 level extends from +2 to +5 V and the 1 level from 0 to +0.8 V.

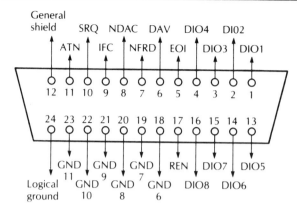

Figure 3.20

If the structure of the IEEE-488 bus and the signals used, as shown in Figure 3.19, are examined, it is possible to distinguish between the following:

- The data bus of eight lines, DIO1–DIO8 (Data In–Out), in which transfers are made in bytes.
- The 'handshaking' bus consisting of three lines: DAV (DAta Valid), NRFD (Not Ready For Data) and NDAC (Not Data ACcepted).
- The control bus consisting of five lines: ATN (ATtentioN), IFC (InterFace Clear), which allows the computer to take precedence over other units, EOI (End Or Identify), REN (Remote ENable), SRQ (Service ReQuest).

The units connected to the bus can be 'talkers', which are only transmitters, 'listeners', which only receive, or a combination of the two. One of the last type must be the unit that manages the whole system – the controller that is the central processing unit of the computer. It must be emphasized that at a given time there must be only one active talker on the system and the conversation between talker and listener(s) continues without intervention by the controller once the latter has designated the transmitter and receiver(s).

Table 3.3

Bit	7	6	5	4	3	2	1	0
Control bus	X	0	0	C	C	C	C	C
Receiver address	X	0	1	L	L	L	L	L
Transmitter address	X	1	0	T	T	T	T	T
Secondary address	X	1	1	S	S	S	S	S

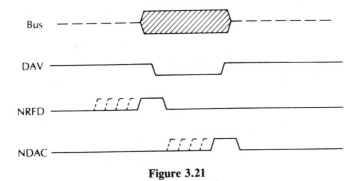

Figure 3.21

As previously mentioned, it is the controller that takes care of the addressing of units. To realize this operation, it transmits a byte containing:

- 1 possible parity bit (bit 7).
- 5 address bits (bits 0, 1, 2, 3 and 4).
- 2 bits specifying the mode of operation (bits 5 and 6).

Addressing is at two levels: a primary level that corresponds to a simple function, and a secondary level that relates to an extended function and allows addressing of subsystems of units. This is represented in Table 3.3 (C = Control, T = Talker, L = Listener, S = Secondary). A timing diagram showing the handshaking exchange protocol is given in Figure 3.21.

When a device requests a service, it sets the SRQ line to 1 in order to attract the attention of the controller; this can ignore the request as long as it wishes. When the request is accepted, the controller must clearly know which unit initiated it. There are two methods for this:

- Successive interrogation of each unit.
- Parallel interrogation (eight units at the most at one time).

In the first case, the controller sets ATN to 1 and the addressed device indicates its present state; 8 bits of data are available for this operation. In the second situation, the controller sets ATN and EOI to 1; each unit indicates, using a single bit, whether or not it initiated the SRQ signal. The latter method clearly has the advantage of speed (eight units can be interrogated simultaneously) but the information that can be transmitted by each device concerning its state is clearly reduced to the simplest, since only a single response bit is available.

Chapter 4

Serial links

4.1 General considerations

These links are used when the transmission distance exceeds 1–2 meters. They are also obligatory when use is made of telephone lines, optical fibers, radio links, communication satellites and so on. In these situations 'modems', in which a carrier wave is modulated by the signal to be transmitted and demodulated in order to extract the useful information, must be used at each end of the transmission channel. This equipment will be discussed again later in this chapter.

4.2 Synchronous serial links

Within serial transmission, this mode of operation permits the highest transmission speeds, generally above 9,600 baud. Synchronous links are intended for transmission of data in the form of blocks that can contain several thousands of characters. Each message is preceded by transmission of information intended to synchronize the receiver with the transmitter within its limits. As mentioned in Chapter 1, either the transmitter and receiver have a common clock whose signal is transmitted by a separate wire, or the timing information is sent via the modem.

The error-detecting code most commonly used in synchronous transmission is the CRC discussed in Chapter 2. There are two types of protocol for synchronous links: the byte-oriented byte control protocol (BCP) such as IBM's Bisync and the bit oriented protocol (BOP). A typical structure of a packet transmitted in BCP is given in Figure 4.1.

| Sync. | Sync. | Sync. | Header | Message | CRC |

Figure 4.1

This includes the synchronizing characters (there are often two) that have already been mentioned and can be sent continuously, even in the absence of data to be transmitted. These characters must be chosen in such a way that they cannot be confused with a useful character or a group of random bits. Note again the header that generally contains control information and often an indication of the total number of bytes in the block, the useful information called the 'message' and the check bits (CRC).

Bit oriented protocols are the most recently developed and provide more flexibility than previous protocols; they allow, for example, transmission of data of arbitrary length. The contents of a BOP type packet are given in Figure 4.2. In terms of the structure, the only, relatively minor, difference consists of the 'flag' situated at the beginning of the packet, which is the equivalent of a synchronizing character. As the protocol is bit oriented, this flag very rarely belongs to a character set; it is very often formed from a special sequence of bits.

Flag	Header	Information	CRC	Flag

Figure 4.2

The header and check sections are generally coded in binary rather than in the form of characters from a set.

Recall the existence of the isochronous mode in which each transmitted character is enclosed between start and stop bits and where the time interval between transmission of two successive characters is an exact multiple of the duration of one bit. Synchronization is achieved by the transmitter; transmission speed can reach 9,600 baud.

An overview of the operation of two interfaces suitable for synchronous transmission will now be presented. The first is the Motorola MC6852 Synchronous Serial Data Adaptor (SSDA) designed to operate with a microprocessor such as the 6800 from the same manufacturer. Figure 4.3 shows an arrangement including this interface. The reader will find simplified and detailed block diagrams of the internal structure of this device in Figures 4.4 and 4.5, respectively. This interface has seven internal registers:

- One status register.
- One receiving register whose contents are the received information.
- Three control registers.
- One transmission register containing the data to be transmitted.
- One synchronizing register that contains the synchronizing character used; this register must be loaded by the microprocessor each time power is applied as this resets the device to zero.

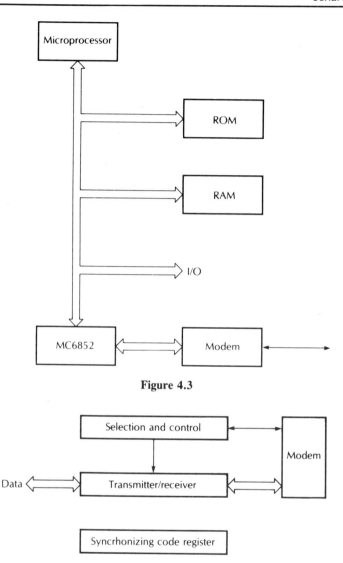

Figure 4.3

Figure 4.4

The data to be transmitted are sent to a first in, first out (FIFO) buffer, which can contain three bytes; information on the status of this buffer is present in the status register. Then the data pass into the transmission shift register where, timed by the transmission clock, the serial to parallel conversion is performed. In the absence of useful data to be transmitted, the FIFO buffer is automatically filled, either with the synchronizing character or with 'ones' in all positions according to the value of a control bit. These 'substitute characters' are inserted into the

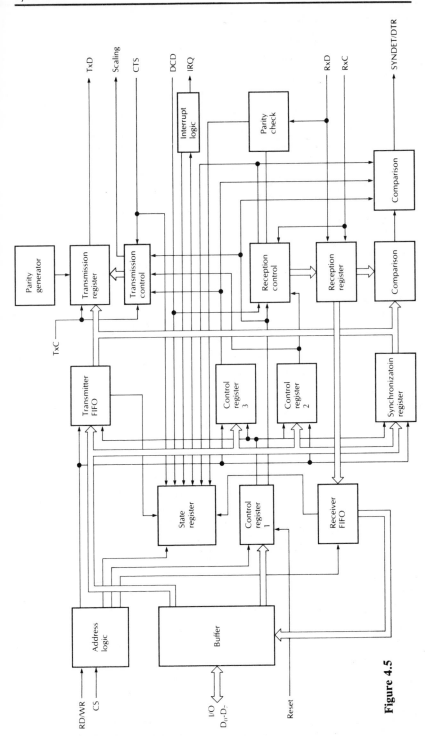

Figure 4.5

transmitted string in such a way that synchronization is not lost. One such state is called 'underflow' and is indicated by sending a pulse on the corresponding line. The 'Clear To Send' line allows for control of the transmitter by an external device such as a modem, for example; the transmitter can thus be inhibited without altering the contents of the FIFO buffer (by means of this line the modem informs the interface that it is ready to send data). At the receiver, the Data Carrier Detection triggers the synchronization process, which can use one or two characters according to the word in the control register. The received characters are compared with the synchronization character and, in the case of agreement, a SYNChronization MATCH pulse is generated on the appropriate line. This line also serves to signal 'Data Terminal Ready', in other words the terminal is under power and operating correctly.

The second device of interest can operate equally well with synchronous and asynchronous communication: it is the Intel 8251A Universal Synchronous–Asynchronous Receiver–Transmitter (USART). In this section, only features relating to synchronous links are of interest; asynchronous operation will be considered in a later section. Figure 4.6 shows the use of a USART in a synchronous communication system using a modem. A simplified block diagram of the internal structure of the device is given in Figure 4.7. Because of the many facilities provided by this interface, its mode of operation is rather complex. Consider firstly the read/write control logic. The chip select signal (CS) ensures selection of the device, the read (RD) and write (WR) signals control read and write operations, respectively. Finally, a Command/Data line allows access to be specified to the data port or the command port which serves to load the internal mode, command and synchronization registers and to read the status register. Examination of the modem control part shows the following outputs:

- DTR – Data Terminal Ready.
- RTS – Request to Send.

The inputs are:

- CTS – Clear to Send (the USART can transmit only if this is at 1).
- DSR – Data Set Ready.

The following outputs are available at the 'transmisson control' stage:

- TxRDY – Transmitter ReaDY the transmitter is ready to accept another character provided by the microprocessor.
- TxE – Transmitter Empty the transmission section has transmitted all the characters sent to the transmitter of the USART.

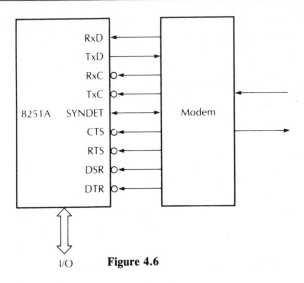

Figure 4.6

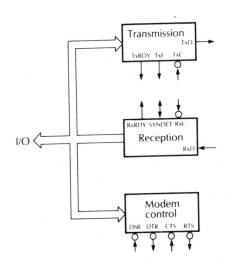

Figure 4.7

There is one input:

• TxC – Transmitter Clock.

There is one output from the 'receiver control' and one input; respectively:

• RxRDY – Receiver ReaDY: at 1 when a character has been received.
• RxC – Receiver Clock.

And one rather special pin in the sense that it has three functions of which only two are relevant to synchronous operation:

- SYNDET – this line can serve as an output which is set to 1 each time a synchronizing character has been detected, or as an input when the synchronizing signal is detected in external devices as is the case when special protocols are used.

As with the interface analyzed previously, this device must also be configured by the microprocessor when power is applied. The appropriate bytes will be written into the control port and access to the required internal register is obtained by means of a pointer. The first register to be initialized is that for the mode; the significance, in synchronous mode, of the bits that it contains are as follows:

- Bit 7 – synchronization over one or two characters.
- Bit 6 – synchronization character detection by external devices or by the internal mechanism of the interface.
- Bit 5 – choice of parity.
- Bit 4 – parity checking.
- Bit 3 – the most significant bit determining the length of characters.
- Bit 2 – the least significant bit determining the length of characters.
- Bit 1 – must be at 0.
- Bit 0 – must be at 0.

Bits 2 and 3 allow the character length to be chosen from 5 to 8 bits. Once this register is loaded, there is no further access to it unless a reset is caused via the RESET pin or via a software procedure. Next the register(s) containing the synchronizing character(s) is loaded. The next step consists of initializing the control register; the effect of the bits is as follows:

- Bit 7 – enter synchronization character search mode (only in synchronous mode).
- Bit 6 – internal reset of the USART (discontinue internal operations and return the pointer to the mode register).
- Bit 5 – RTS (Request To Send).
- Bit 4 – reset to 0 of the status register error bits.
- Bit 3 – put a 'break' signal on the communication line by forcing TxD to the low level.
- Bit 2 – received signal check.
- Bit 1 – DTR (Data Terminal Ready).
- Bit 0 – transmitted signal check.

The status register of the USART can be read via the control port; the bits are:

- Bit 7 – DSR (Data Set Ready).
- Bit 6 – SYNDET.
- Bit 5 – framing error (not used on synchronous mode).
- Bit 4 – overflow error (when a character is received although another is waiting to be read in the receiving register).
- Bit 3 – parity error.
- Bit 2 – TxE (all characters have been sent to the USART transmitter).
- Bit 1 – RxRDY (a character has been received).
- Bit 0 – TxRDY (acceptance of a character from the microprocessor).

4.3 Asynchronous serial links

As shown in a previous chapter, this mode of transmission requires each character to be preceded by start and stop bits. Because of this, the useful part of the transmission becomes rather small. Assuming that characters are sent in the form of bytes that are preceded by a start bit and followed by two stop bits, relevant information represents only 8/11 or 73 percent of the total. Transmission speeds are less than those permitted in synchronous mode; they do not exceed 10 Mbaud. In practice, they are very often much less than this.

The Intel 8251A USART, whose schematic representation is given in Figure 4.7, will be examined. This time attention will be devoted to operation in asynchronous mode. Figure 4.8 shows an arrangement in which the USART is coupled to an asynchronous modem.

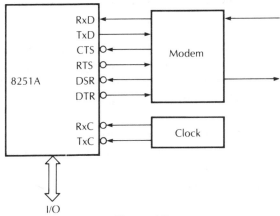

Figure 4.8

From the point of view of the interface connections, only SYNDET has a different function; in asynchronous mode, this line goes to the logic 1 level when the USART receives a break command whose duration exceeds two characters.

In asynchronous mode, the bits of the mode register are defined as follows:

- Bit 7 – most significant bit of the number of stop bits.
- Bit 6 – least significant bit of the number of stop bits.
- Bit 5 – parity selection.
- Bit 4 – parity check.
- Bit 3 – most significant bit determining character length.
- Bit 2 – least significant bit determining character length.
- Bit 1 – most significant bit of the bit rate factor.
- Bit 0 – least significant bit of the bit rate factor.

The valid combinations for bits 1 and 0 are:

> 01   bit rate = clock frequency.
> 10   bit rate = clock frequency/16.
> 11   bit rate = clock frequency/64.

Notice that only a single start bit can be used.

The bits of the command register are the same as in synchronous mode except that bit 7 is not used. Similarly for the state register, bit 5 operates only in asynchronous mode and is set to the specified value on reception of a character without stop bits.

4.4 The RS-232C (EIA) and V.24 (CCITT) standards and derivatives

The RS-232C specification, which is the most commonly used for serial transmission, was drawn up by the American Electronic Industry Association (EIA). It is very similar to the V.24 standard developed by the International Telegraph and Telephone Consultative Committee (CCITT).

These standards make use of negative logic:

- The 0 level corresponds to voltages between +5 and +25 V (+15 V on load).
- The 1 level corresponds to voltages between −5 and −25 V (−15 V on load).

It follows that there is no direct TTL compatibility; level converters must be used.

According to the RS-232C standard, the length of cable cannot exceed about fifteen meters. In practice, however, links of thirty and even sixty meters are often realized without difficulty. The transmission speed is limited to 20 kbaud.

the equipment divides into two categories:

- Data Terminal Equipment (DTE).
- Data Communication Equipment (DCE).

This distinction is purely arbitrary and usually left to the discretion of the manufacturer. When a modem is incorporated in a link, it will be the 'DCE' and the device to which it is connected (for example, a computer, a terminal or a printer) becomes the 'DTE'. In the case of a direct link between, for example, a computer and a terminal, the situation is not very clearly defined. This problem will be examined again later.

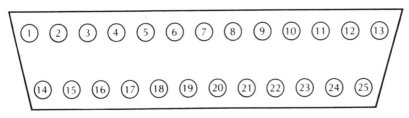

Figure 4.9

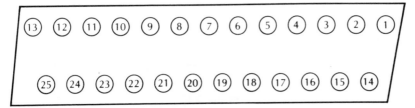

Figure 4.10

Figures 4.9 and 4.10 show the pin connections for RS-232C and V.24 connectors respectively and Table 4.1 lists the various signals. From this it follows that the 'DTE' transmits on terminal 2 and receives on terminal 3 while the 'DCE' transmits on terminal 3 and receives on terminal 2. Figure 4.11 shows the connections necessary for serial transmission between a 'DTE' and a 'DCE'; these include those that have already been mentioned and connection of the common logic ground. In this configuration, signals for controlling the exchange

Table 4.1

Pin	Standard		Source		Designation	
	V.24 CCITT	RS-232C EIA	DTE	DCE		Abbr.
1	101	AA			Earth Ground	–
2	103	BA	●		Transmitted Data	TD
3	104	BB		●	Received Data	RD
4	105	CA	●		Request to Send	RTS
5	106	CB		●	Clear To Send	CTS
6	107	CC		●	Data Set Ready	DSR
7	102	AA			Logic Ground	–
8	109	CF		●	Carrier Detect	RLSD
9	–	–			Reserved	–
10	–	–			Reserved	–
11	126	–	●		Unassigned	–
12	122	SCF		●	Secondary Carrier Detect	RLSD
13	121	SCB		●	Secondary Clear to Send	CTS
14	118	SBA	●		Secondary Transmitted Data	TD
15	114	DB		●	Transmit Clock	–
16	119	SBB		●	Secondary Received Data	RD
17	115	DD		●	Receiver Clock	–
18	141	–	●		Unassigned	–
19	120	SCA	●		Secondary Request to Send	RTS
20	108/1	–	●		Data Terminal Ready	CDSL
	108/2	CD	●			DTR
21	140	–	●		Signal Quality Detect	–
22	125	CE		●	Ring Detect	RI
23	111	CH	●		Data Rate Select	–
24	113	DA	●		Transmit Clock	–
25	142	–		●	Unassigned	–

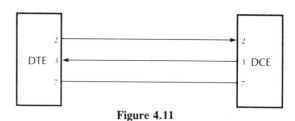

Figure 4.11

process are not provided. In the majority of practical cases, at least two signals must be added in order to support an exchange that uses 'handshaking'; these are as follows:

- DSR (Data Set Ready) – data equipment ready, set to 1 by the DCE to indicate that it is under power and operating correctly.
- RTS (Request To Send) – transmission request by the DTE.

There are also the equivalent signals:

- DTR (Data Terminal Ready) – the equivalent of DSR for the DTE.

- DCD (Data Carrier Detection) – carrier detection.
- CTS (Clear To Send) – initiated by the DCE when the link is established.

The other RS-232C lines and the secondary channel, which is practically unused in asynchronous mode, are of less importance and will not be discussed here. A protocol of the type used for the establishment of a link could, for example, consist of the following actions:

- Activation of DTR by the DTE.
- Activation of DSR by the DCE.
- Activation of DCD by the DCE to indicate that it has detected the carrier of the other modem.
- Activation of RTS by the DTE.
- Activation of CTS by the DCE.

When a link between two DTEs or two DCEs must be realized, it is necessary to cross certain lines and this is achieved by means of a special cable called a 'null modem cable'. Figure 4.12 shows an example for the case of two DTEs.

Arising from the RS-232C standard, other specifications have been developed to avoid, to some extent, the limitations imposed by RS-232C: these are RS-422, RS-423 and RS-449. These three standards are related: RS-449 specifies the logic signal definitions while the electrical levels to be observed are specified by RS-423 for common mode operation and by RS-422 for differential mode. Table 4.2 shows the various RS-449 signals with their RS-232C equivalents.

From this table, the appearance of ten new signals can be noted:

- Send Common – logical ground of the data transmission line of the DTE.
- Receive Common – logical ground of the data transmission line of the DCE.
- Terminal in Service – initiated by the DTE to signal that it is operational (for example, in the case of a busy intelligent terminal).

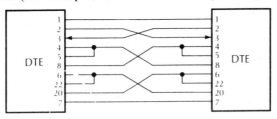

Figure 4.12

Table 4.2

Function	EIA RS-449 name	RS-232C equivalent
Common	Signal Ground	Signal Ground
	Transmitter Common	–
	Receiver Common	–
Control	Terminal in Service	Ring Indicator
	Incoming Call	Data Terminal Ready
	Terminal Ready	Data Set Ready
	Data Mode	
Primary channel		
Data	Data Transmission	Data Transmission
	Data Reception	Data Reception
Synchronization	Terminal Synchronization	External Transmission Clock
	Send Synchronization	Transmission Clock
	Receiver Synchronization	Receiver Clock
Control	Request To Send	Request To Send
	Clear To Send	Clear To Send
	Receiver Ready	Carrier Detection
	Signal Quality	Signal Quality Detection
	New Signal	–
	Select Frequency	–
	Select Rate	Select Rate[a]
	Rate Indication	Select Rate[a]
Secondary channel		
Data	Secondary Data Transmission	Secondary Data Transmission
	Secondary Data Reception	Secondary Data Reception
Control	Secondary Request To Send	Secondary Request To Send
	Secondary Clear To Send	Secondary Clear To Send
	Secondary Receiver Ready	Secondary Carrier Detector
Others		
Control	Local Loopback	–
	Remote Loopback	–
	Test Mode	–
	Select Standby	–
	Standby Indicator	–

[a] With RS-232C the rate selection signal can be provided or generated by the DTE. RS-449 has two signals, one for each direction.

- New Signal – initiated by the DTE when it requires the DCE to prepare to establish a link.
- Select Frequency – in the case of full duplex links, each modem modulates a carrier of different frequency (frequency division multiplexing); from this signal, the DTE can select the required frequency from the two available to the DCE.
- Local Loopback – this is initiated by the DTE and causes looping of the DCE transmitter to the receiver of the DTE communication channel; in this way the DCE can be tested by monitoring transmitted and received messages.

- Remote Loopback – this is initiated by the DTE and causes connection by the DCE of the send and receive lines at the remote end of the link; in this way a test loop is formed by checking the agreement of transmitted and received messages.
- Test Mode – indicates to the DTE that the DCE is in test mode.
- Emergency Selection – initiated by the DTE to request the use of an emergency communication channel as far as hardware redundancy permits.
- Emergency Indicator – indicates to the DTE when emergency devices are being used for communication.

The performance of the RS-232C standard is limited by the high peak-to-peak voltages and short rise times, which are sources of cross-talk on the lines, the use of a single ground line and other factors; the RS-422 and RS-423 specifications were formulated to reduce these disadvantages. Several ground lines are now available and the signal amplitudes have been restricted:

- The 0 level corresponds to voltages between +200 mV and +6 V.
- The 1 level corresponds to voltages between −200 mV and −6 V.

The RS-423 standard requires the use of a single line, compatible with the RS-232C standard. In contrast, the RS-422 specification recommends the use of a differential line consisting of two wires, each in the opposite logical state; the voltage between them is double that in the case of a single line. Tables 4.3(a) and (b) give the pin connections of the two connectors of 37 and 9 pins, respectively, required by the RS-449 Standard; Table 4.4 summarizes the standards that have already been examined in a similar way.

4.5 Modems

When it is required to transmit digital data over distances greater than a kilometer, the simplest method is to make use of the telephone network. Because of its basic role, this is suitable for transmission of voice signals in a frequency band from approximately 300 to 3,300 Hz and not digital signals. This makes it necessary to use an *adaptor*; this is a modem (MOdulator–DEModulator) whose principle of operation has been outlined previously. At the transmitter, a carrier of frequency between 300 and 3,300 Hz will be modulated by the signal to be transmitted, while at the receiver this same carrier is demodulated in such a way as to extract the useful information. With full duplex

Table 4.3(a)

Pin	Signal name
1	Shield
2	Signal Rate Indicator
3	Spare
4	Send Data
5	Send Timing
6	Receive Data
7	Request To Send
8	Receive Timing
9	Clear To Send
10	Local Loopback
11	Data Mode
12	Terminal Ready
13	Receiver Ready
14	Remote Loopback
15	Incoming Call
16	Select Signaling Rate/Select Frequency
17	Terminal Timing
18	Test Mode
19	Signal Ground
20	Receive Common
21	Spare
22	Send Data (common or differential)
23	Send Timing (common or differential)
24	Receive Data (common or differential)
25	Request To Send (common or differential
26	Receive Timing (common or differential)
27	Clear To Send (common or differential)
28	Terminal In Service
29	Data Mode (common or differential)
30	Terminal Ready (common or differential)
31	Receiver Ready (common or differential)
32	Select Standby
33	Signal Quality
34	New Signal
35	Terminal Timing (common or differential)
36	Standby Indicator
37	Send Common

Note The signals indicated as common or differential are common for RS-423A and constitute one of the two wires of the differential pair for RS-422A. The signals that do not have two pins assigned to their function must be operated with RS-423A amplifiers and receivers.

communication, frequency division multiplexing is used; each of the two modems uses a carrier of different frequency and this indicates that two carrier frequencies are available within the modem. In the case of synchronous communication, the clock information can also be provided by the modem. Modems connected to the switched telephone network are used as follows: the number of the telephone to be called is dialed on a conventional telephone and when communication is established, the

Table 4.3(b)

Pin	Signal name
1	Shield
2	Secondary Receiver Ready
3	Secondary Send Data
4	Secondary Receive Data
5	Signal Ground
6	Receive Common (for secondary channel)
7	Secondary Request To Send
8	Secondary Clear To Send
9	Send Common (for secondary channel)

Table 4.4

Characteristics	RS-232C	RS-423	RS-422
Data mode	One wire	One wire	Differential
Max. cable length			
Feet	50	2,000	4,000
Meters	17	666	1,333
Max. rate (kbaud)	20	300	10,000
Max. open circuit output voltage (V)	±25	±6	6 differential
Min. on load output voltage (V)	±5 to ±15	±3.6	2 differential
Min. output R (Ω) or current (μA)	$R_0 = 300\ \Omega$	100 μA from -6 to $+6$ V	$-100\ \mu$A from $+6$ to 0.25 V
Max. short circuit current (mA)	±500	±150	±150
Max. receiver threshold (V)	-3 to $+3$	-0.2 to $+0.2$	-0.2 to $+0.2$
Max. receiver input voltage (V)	-25 to $+25$	-12 to $+12$	-12 to $+12$

link to the telephone is switched to the modem by means of a relay. Facilities for automatic calling may also be available. The called modem normally makes use of an automatic answering device which, on receipt of a call, automatically switches the line from the telephone to the modem.

For completeness, acoustic couplers should be mentioned; these are an economic form of modem in the strict sense. Their principal difference lies in the fact that they are coupled to the telephone line acoustically and not electrically; the digital data is converted into an acoustic signal, usually by means of frequency modulation. The main disadvantage of these devices is their low speed – from 110 to 1,800 baud.

The various types of modulation used by modems will now be examined. The carrier can be modulated in three fundamentally different ways: in amplitude, in frequency and in phase. These forms of modulation may possibly be combined with each other. The basic concepts will be briefly reviewed.

The principle of *amplitude modulation* (AM) is illustrated in Figures 4.13 and 4.14. The first of these two figures represents modulation where two amplitudes are possible and correspond to logical 0 and 1; this is the *amplitude shift keying* (ASK) mode. The second figure relates to a situation where four amplitudes are available each of which corresponds to one of the pairs of bits 00, 01, 10 and 11. In this way the bit rate can be doubled while retaining the same transmission speed. There is no *a priori* reason why the number of working levels should not be further increased. Examination of the frequency spectrum occupied by amplitude modulation shows that there is redundancy; if ω is the carrier frequency, the frequency band used extends from $\omega - \Delta\omega$ to $\omega + \Delta\omega$ where $2\Delta\omega$ represents the bandwidth. In order to recover the information, it is sufficient to consider either the $\omega - \Delta\omega$ or the $\omega + \Delta\omega$ part; hence the necessary bandwidth can be halved. This is achieved by filtering and in this way *single side band* (SSB) modulation is obtained. The major disadvantage of amplitude modulation is its high sensitivity to noise.

Frequency modulation (FM) will now be considered. Its principle is illustrated in Figure 4.15 for the case where two frequencies corresponding to logical 0 and 1, respectively, are used; this is the *frequency shift keying* (FSK) mode. As with amplitude modulation, four or more frequencies may be used. As an illustrative example, CCITT Note V.21 recommends the frequencies to be used for 200-baud modems; for asynchronous FSK in full duplex, the carriers are 1,080 and 1,750 Hz, respectively, with a frequency deviation of ± 100 Hz, hence the frequencies will be 980 and 1,180 Hz for one channel and 1,650 and 1,850 Hz for the other.

In conclusion, it should be noted that frequency modulation is more resistant to noise than amplitude modulation but requires a wider bandwidth.

The last type of modulation to be reviewed is *phase modulation* (PM) whose principle is illustrated in Figure 4.16 for the case where phase shifts of 0° and 180° correspond to logical 0 and 1; this is the *differential phase shift keying* (DPSK) mode. Again, more than four phases can be used. Phase modulation is now tending to supersede the two other types of modulation since it is very insensitive to noise and is well suited to high-speed transmission, above 2,000 baud.

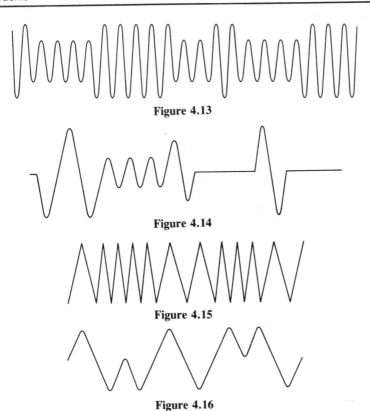

Figure 4.13

Figure 4.14

Figure 4.15

Figure 4.16

To conclude this section devoted to modems, some relevant CCITT Notes will be listed:

1. *Interfaces*

    V.24   Definition of circuits for exchanges between modems and terminals

    V.25   Automatic calling and/or replying equipment and inhibition of echo suppressors

2. *Modems for leased lines*

    V.22b Standardization of bit rates

    V.26   2,400-baud modems

    V.27   4,800-baud modems

    V.29   4,800/9,600-baud modems

3. *Modems for the switched network*

    V.15   Acoustic coupling

    V.21   200-baud modems

    V.22   Standardization of bit rates

    V.23   600/1,200-baud modems

    V.26b 1,200/2,400-baud modems

Chapter 5

Data processing networks: interconnection equipment and standards

5.1 Equipment organization

Fundamentally, a data processing network consists of computers and peripherals. The latter are not generally continuously active and consequently it would not be economic to assign a high-capacity transmission line to each one. When there are many of them, it is preferable to adopt the structure of Figure 5.1, where low-capacity links connect the peripherals to either a *(de)multiplexer* or a *concentrator* and hence to a high-capacity line. This equipment must manage the transmission and operation of the peripherals, particularly their multiplexing. Originally, the essential difference between (de)multiplexers and concentrators lay in the fact that the latter were specialized computers that performed preprocessing, information storage, protection

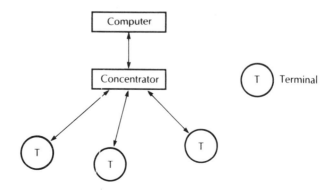

Figure 5.1

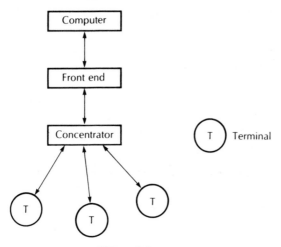

Figure 5.2

management and so on, while the (de)multiplexers consisted solely of wired logic. With the development of microprocessor technology, this difference has blurred considerably and programmable (de)multiplexers are now available. Control of all these devices is generally realized by the *communications controller unit* (CCU) of the computer. However, the use of a *front end processor* (FEP) allows the computer to be freed from the task of communication management; this is illustrated in Figure 5.2.

One of the fundamental operations performed by both concentrators and multiplexers is that of multiplexing; the *transmission channel* is divided into *sub-channels* associated with different peripherals. There are three essential types of multiplexing:

- *Frequency division multiplexing* (FDM), which can be used when the transmission medium has a sufficiently wide bandwidth; this is possible for telephone lines without loading coils (only amplifiers are present on the line), wideband coaxial cables, optical fibres and so on. A frequency that is subjected to modulation is associated with each sub-channel (as in the case of full duplex links using modems).
- *Time division multiplexing* (TDM) where a certain fraction of the time is reserved for each sub-channel.
- *Statistical* or *demand multiplexing*, which is a variant of TDM where the sub-channels are allocated as a function of the volume of information to be transmitted; this necessitates the use of buffer memories and destination indications. At the present time, the use of frequency division multiplexing is very much reduced with respect to the other two.

5.2 Interconnection standards

For system interconnection, use is made of standards that permit information exchange between terminals, computers, networks, individuals, processes and so on. This led to the announcement by IBM in 1974 of its Systems Network Architecture (SNA), which consists of a set of conventions internal to the company.

As interconnection must be available to all types of hardware and exchange, the International Standards Organization (ISO) has defined the Open Systems Interconnection (OSI) standards, which provide seven layers as indicated in Figure 5.3.

The significance of these layers is as follows:

- *Physical layer* – provides the interface with the physical support of transmission (telephone lines, fiber optics, and so on).
- *Data link layer* – uses the circuits of the physical layer to provide error free transmission of information.
- *Network layer* – provides possible routing of data through a network of intermediate systems.
- *Transport layer* – provides the transport functions from one end of the chain to the other by using the services provided by the network in an optimum manner.
- *Session layer* – provides the functions of establishing and controlling the dialogs between entities of the presentation layer.
- *Presentation layer* – provides manipulation of data structures (formatting, checking, and so on).
- *Application layer* – corresponds to the functions performed by distributed applications (including programs, physical devices, human operators, and so on).

Using similar concepts, the IEEE has undertaken the specification of standards for the use of *local area networks* (LANs); these are the IEEE-802 specifications, which are based on a less global outlook in the

7 Application
6 Presentation
5 Session
4 Transport
3 Network
2 Data link
1 Physical

Figure 5.3

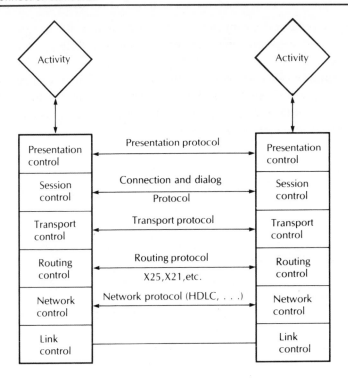

Figure 5.4

sense that they have been divided into different parts and they cover only the two lower levels of the OSI standards. The list is as follows:

802.2   logical monitoring of the link.
802.3   use of the *carrier sense multiple access/collision detection* (CSMA/CD) protocol.
802.4   use of a *token bus* structure.
802.5   use of a *token ring* structure.

All these concepts will be described in the sections devoted to protocols and local area networks.

The CCITT has established standard X.25 for *packet switching*, which will be treated later and covers the three lower layers of the OSI recommendations.

CII-Honeywell Bull has developed a structure in response to the OSI standards which is represented in Figure 5.4; it is the *Distributed Systems Architecture*. This architecture permits access to the resources of a computer using any terminal, independently of any particular feature, and common connection of equipment at different processing centres.

Certain protocols which have already been described correspond to the three lower layers of the OSI standards; for example, the RS-232C and RS-449 Standards for the physical layer. The other protocols will be described subsequently in this work.

Chapter 6

Protocols

6.1 Introduction

It was seen in Chapter 5 that interconnection standards are divided into layers with different corresponding protocols. These will be reviewed in relation to the physical and data link layers.

6.2 Physical layer standards

These will be treated very briefly. The specifications used are the RS-232C, RS-422, RS-423, RS-449 etc. standards, which have already been thoroughly described in the chapter devoted to serial transmission.

6.3 Data link layer standards

6.3.1 Introduction

At this level, typical protocols are the IBM *Bisync* (*Binary Synchronous Communications* (BSC)), the *Synchronous Data Link Control* (SDLC) from the same company, the *Digital Data Communication Message Protocol* (DDCMP) from Digital Equipment, the *High Level Data Link Control* (HDLC) by ISO, and so on. These will now be reviewed.

6.3.2 The IBM Bisync (BSC)

This procedure can be applied to synchronous links, point-to-point or multipoint, which are operated in half duplex, that is alternately. It is for medium- and high-speed transmissions from 600 baud; this is the reason for choosing the synchronous mode.

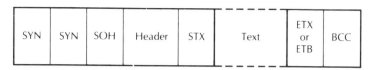

Figure 6.1

Figure 6.1 shows the structure of a message in BSC. Examination of this frame shows that a message consists, in the order of reception, of the following:

- Two synchronization characters: SYN.
- A header statement (optional): *Start Of Header*.
- An optional header.
- A start of text statement: *Start of TeXt*.
- The text consisting of ASCII, EBCDIC or 6-bit coded characters.
- An end-of-block or end-of-text character: *End of Transmission Block* or *End of TeXt*.
- A monitoring character: *Block Check Character*; in ASCII longitudinal and vertical checks are used while in EBCDIC and 6-bit codes, CRC is used.

The principal command characters are as follows:

- ETB (*End of Transmission Block*) indicates the end of a block of characters whose start is represented by SOH (*Start Of Header*) or STX (*Start of TeXt*); the receiver is required to provide a response as to its state.
- ETX (*End of Text*) is similar to ETB but also indicates that there are no more blocks of data to be transmitted.
- DLE (*Data Link Escape*) forms transparent message frames and is associated with STX, ETX, ETB and so on. The concept of transparency must be used when it is required to transmit messages containing characters that could be confused with delimiters and must not be treated as such. When it is itself part of the transparent data, DLE must be duplicated to avoid all possibility of confusion.
- ITB (*end of InTermediate Block*) separates messages into sections for error detection and precedes a test block; the receiver checks the latter but responds only after reception of an ETB or an ETX. These intermediate blocks are enclosed by DLE STX and DLE ETB or DLE ETX, thereby making the transmitted data transparent.
- ENQ (*ENQiry*) signals the end of an equipment polling operation or selection in multipoint operation. It also serves to request an ACK or NAK acknowledgment again.

- EOT (*End Of Transmission*) signals the end of transmission of blocks of data; during equipment polling it is the response for 'Nothing to transmit'.
- ACK (0,1) (*ACKnowledge*) is used alternately as an acknowledgment of correct reception of even and odd order blocks.
- NAK (*Not AcKnowledge*) indicates erroneous reception.
- WACK (*Wait ACKnowledge*) indicates that the receiver is not ready to acknowledge reception; the transmitter will send ENQs to which it will respond with WACK until the receiver is ready.
- RVI (*ReVerse Interrupt*) is a reception acknowledgment that indicates that the receiver wishes to have priority for its turn to become a transmitter.
- TTD (*Temporary Text Delay*) enables a line to be reserved by the transmitter although it is not ready; the receiver responds with NAK and this exchange of TTD and NAK continues until the start of data transmission.

6.3.3 The IBM Synchronous Data Link Control (SDLC)

This procedure is bit oriented, which makes it perfectly transparent to the form of coding used; the codes can be of any length. The frame of an SDLC message is represented in Figure 6.2. It can be seen that this frame consists of the following:

- Two 'delimiters' or 'flags' that enclose the information; they consist of the bit sequence 01111110. Consequently the same sequence is not permitted elsewhere and this is why a zero is automatically inserted by the transmitter after a sequence of five consecutive 1s (the receiver automatically eliminates this zero).
- An address field that defines the secondary station (monitored station) involved in the exchange.
- A control field that contains the commands intended for the secondary station and the responses sent from it to the primary station.
- A field that contains the sequence of data bits; its length can be zero (no information).
- A *Frame Check Sequence*.

Delimiter	Address	Information	Frame check sequence (FCS)	Delimiter
01111110		Sequence of binary elements		01111110

Figure 6.2

6.3.4 The Digital Equipment Digital Data Communication Message Protocol (DDCMP)

This byte-oriented protocol, proposed by Digital Equipment, is very general; it is suitable for links that may be synchronous or asynchronous, full or half duplex (alternate), point-to-point or multipoint and serial or parallel. The structure of a message is illustrated in Figure 6.3. It can be seen that a message consists of the following:

- Two synchronization characters: SYN.
- A field that defines the class of message; data, command or maintenance which correspond to the special characters *Start Of Header*, *ENQuiry* and *Data Link Escape* respectively.
- A 14-bit counter block that indicates, in data mode, the number of data characters; in command mode it specifies the order. In the case of a negative acknowledgment 'NAK', it specifies the type of error detected (buffer unavailable, speed too high, message too long, and so on).
- Two indicators: Q (*Quick sync*), which indicates to the receiver that the message will be followed by synchronization characters, and S (*Select*), which signifies to the receiver that the transmitter has reached the last message.
- A response block that contains the order number of the last correctly received character (each message is divided into strings of 256 characters for checking).
- A sequence block that, in data mode, contains the order number of the sequence; in command mode, it enables the transmitter to interrogate the receiver.
- An address field that permits selection of a station in multipoint operation.
- A header checking field using 16-bit CRC.
- The data.
- A data check field also using 16-bit CRC.

S Y N	S Y N	C L A S S	Counter (14 bits)	I n d i c a t o r s	2 b i t s	Response (8 bits)	Sequence (8 bits)	Address (8 bits)	CRC1 (16 bits)	Message	CRC2 (16 bits)

Figure 6.3

In the case of erroneous reception of a message, a negative acknowledgment NAK is produced; as the order number of the last correct character received is known, the message is retransmitted from this.

6.3.5 The ISO High Level Data Link Control (HDLC)

This protocol is bit oriented, like the IBM SDLC, and is very similar; the structure of a message is given in Figure 6.4. The message frame consists of the following:

- Two 'delimiters' or 'flags' that enclose the information; they consist of the bit sequence 01111110. Consequently this sequence is not permitted elsewhere and this is why a zero is automatically inserted by the transmitter after a sequence of five consecutive 1s (the receiver will automatically eliminate this zero).
- An address field that defines the secondary station (monitored station) involved in the exchange. If the lowest weight bit is at 1, the address contains only a single byte, otherwise it extends to several.
- A command field that contains the commands intended for the secondary station and the responses from it sent to the primary station (the station having control of the link). The address command can contain more than 1 byte.
- A field that contains the sequence of data bits; its length can be zero (no information).
- A *Frame Check Sequence* based on the use of a 16-bit CRC.

Delimiter	Address	Control	Information	Frame check sequence (FCS)	Delimiter
01111110	1 byte or (n bytes)	1 byte or (n bytes)	Sequence of binary elements	2 bytes	01111110

Figure 6.4

Consider the command field. Three transmission formats are possible:

- The information format (I), which is used for the transfer of data. Each frame is numbered; the command field is provided with a modulo 2^p ($p = 3$ or 7) counter of p bits, which gives the number of the transmitted frame at the transmitter, and a second counter for the receiver, which indicates the number of the next awaited frame.
- The supervision format (S), which allows the usual functions to be provided (*ACKnowledgment* of reception, (re)transmission of a frame from a given number (*REJect*), (re)transmission of a single frame (*Selective REJect*), *Receiver Ready*, *Receiver Not Ready* and so on).

- The non-sequential format (N) which defines additional supervisory functions (*Set Asynchronous Response Mode*, *DISConnect*, *CoMmand Reject*, and so on).

One bit is common to these three formats; this is the P/F bit (*Poll/ Final*). Typically, the primary station sends a number of frames with the P/F bit at 0; when it has finished, it sends a frame with the P/F bit at 1 to the secondary station. The secondary station then knows that a response is required and in its turn it will normally send a series of frames with the P/F bit at 0.

In conclusion, notice again that the ISO protocol is divided into different sections: the IS 3309-2 Standards for the structure of the frames, IS 4335 for the detail of the elements of the procedure and DIS 6159 and 6256 for particular operations.

Chapter 7

Information routing

7.1 Algorithms

When using switched telephone networks, or any other network that makes use of 'circuit switching', the choice of route is determined during establishment of communication according to the arrangements for managing the circuits concerned. In contrast, when networks of the 'data switching' type are used, for example 'packet switching' (in which the message to be transmitted is divided into portions called 'packets'), two possibilities are available: either the algorithm determines a route for each packet individually, or the path is fixed for a sequence of packets.

In any case, the complexity of the problem of routing is very strongly linked to the topology of the network. In a star network with full duplex links, all nodes are connected to a central node through which the information to be transmitted must pass and hence only this node must have data on the topology of the network. Each destination node is served by a unique link, and a table relating destination and communication channel can be established.

When the network has a ring structure with full duplex links between the nodes, the messages pass from one to the other until they arrive at their destination. A 'brute force' solution involves not using tables for route determination, in this case it is clear that the path followed will not necessarily be the shortest. The remedy is simple: provide each node with a table that defines the shortest route for each destination or number the nodes to permit calculation of the shortest path. The latter method is also well suited to an algorithm for the determination of routes for regular rectangular mesh networks; the nodes are represented by the numbers of the column and row of which they form the intersection. In the case of a tree structure, the address is sufficient to specify the route to be followed.

All the topologies that have been mentioned, and which lead to simple solutions to the problem of routing information, are very rarely used in reality; most often the structures concerned are irregular. The situation then becomes rather complex and a detailed study of the algorithms used exceeds the scope of this work. It will simply be noted that recourse is frequently made to a hierarchical approach to the network (see Chapter 1). In addition, routing algorithms can be classified according to McQuillan (1974) as follows:

- *Deterministic routing* – according to a fixed policy, not affected by changing conditions.
- *Isolated adaptive routing* – at each node, decisions concerning routing are taken on the basis of purely local information.
- *Distributed adaptive routing* – in this case the nodes exchange information and the routing decisions are taken as a function of local and shared information.
- *Centralized adaptive routing* – the nodes send local information to a central point which in return provides them with routing instructions.

In addition to isolated, distributed and centralized adaptive routing, the work of Rudin (1976) introduces a new class – hybrid adaptive routing, which is a combination of the three. It should again be mentioned that in the case of a packet switching network consisting of an irregular mesh, it is possible to avoid the use of formal routing algorithms, either because the topology of the network is insufficiently known at each node or because this topology is subject to modification (for example, a military network subject to an enemy attack). In this case, the packets can be transmitted by 'flooding' or 'inundation' (multiple copies are sent on all paths leaving the node) or by *random routing* (a single copy of the packet is sent by a link chosen in a random manner).

Generally, the choice of algorithm implemented is made on the basis of simulation of operation of the network based on a mathematical representation.

7.2 Congestion

Problems of congestion arise when the available physical resources are inadequate for the needs of users. This can arise when using concentrators if the output channel is required to exceed its maximum capacity as a consequence of an excessive number of active inputs. A similar situation is possible in the case of *demand multiplexing*; since several units may wish to transmit simultaneously, it is necessary to provide buffer memories in order to store their messages temporarily while waiting for a free communication channel. Consequently, if the number of buffers proves to be insufficient with respect to the volume of messages, a congestion problem arises. In packet switching networks, buffers are also provided at various nodes and, if the number of these memories becomes too small with respect to the data flow, the congestion phenomenon appears. In these networks, this can also result from too small a transmission channel capacity, but this case rarely occurs; congestion problems are usually associated with free buffers.

7.3 Switching

The topic of switching in networks reserved for transmission of data in digital form (specialized networks that may or may not be public) will be tackled here. There are two categories of switching – circuit switching and data switching, and the latter is itself subdivided into message switching and packet switching.

7.3.1 Circuit switching

As with the telephone, this technique consists of physically connecting the transmitting and receiving stations for the duration of effective data communication between them. Taken to the extreme, a new link could be established for the transmission of each character. The result is that these networks require an infrastructure of complex switches that makes them very expensive. Circuit switching is well suited to the telephone, for which the passband and call duration are reasonably uniform; this justifies the cost of these networks. In the case of data transmission this does not apply since the topology of traffic and transmission speeds differ very greatly. With circuit switching, information is treated as a flow of bits that follow each other at a fixed speed, although in reality the exchange of data between computers and terminals should be considered as a sequence of messages. Another disadvantage of circuit switching lies in the fact that it is essential to wait until a free path is found between the dispatcher and the destination before transmission is able to start. The sole advantage of these networks is their small and constant transmission delay.

For all these reasons, attention has turned above all to data switching, although the technology of these networks was well known from telephony. Nevertheless, some countries of Northern Europe have opted for this solution.

7.3.2 Message switching

In the case of message switching, the messages are sent to switching centers or nodes where they may be stored while waiting for a communication channel to be available to route them further. There is not, as in the case of circuit switching, a simultaneous permanent link between the transmitter of the message and its final destination (there is no interaction between them). Also, unlike the latter, there is no risk at a peak period (except in the case of congestion and/or complete blocking of all or part of the network) of not obtaining a link; the messages will be put in memory and delivered after a certain delay, which is insignificant up to 80 percent of the system capacity unless messages of excessive length overload the network. This is the principal reason for changing to packet switching, in which messages are divided into portions or packets.

7.3.3 Packet switching

This technique makes use of the division of messages into portions called packets. The latter are routed from node to node to their final destination; storage may be required at a node if no output communication channel is free.

There are two approaches to packet communication; they make use of the concepts of datagrams and virtual circuits, respectively. Datagrams are packets that contain source and destination information and are treated independently of each other. Consequently, their order of arrival can be different from that of departure. In the case of virtual circuits, a circuit that does not consist of a fixed physical link is created between two *Data Terminal Equipments* (DTEs) situated at each end of the communication channel. These circuits can be permanent (*permanent virtual circuits* (PVCs)), that is established permanently, or switched (*virtual calls* (VCs)), in other words established and canceled on the initiative of a correspondent by connection and disconnection messages, respectively. The same terminal equipment can control several communications on a single connecting link by assigning a logical channel number to each one; this is repeated in the header of the transmitted packets and enables them to be distinguished. For permanent circuits this number alone serves to identify the link used. Virtual circuits also have the property that the order of succession of packets is the same on arrival as on departure; this may involve the cost of using additional equipment when the routing algorithm is partly or totally adaptive.

The links used can be realized physically using cable or radio, for example via satellites. It is not without interest to make this distinction in order to treat the problem of collisions between packets when more than one station starts to transmit at the same instant. In the case of cabled links, all stations are able to listen to each other and this is not necessarily true for radio links (for example, a station situated out of range of some of the others).

One of the foremost packet switching systems from which a large part of the present technology has developed is the Aloha network developed by a group at the University of Hawaii, which became operational in 1970. This network consists of a set of radio stations operating on UHF and distributed throughout the various Hawaiian islands; the choice of radio links resulted essentially from the poor quality of the telephone network in that region. A central communication processing unit through which all packets pass was installed at Menehune. Initially, the transmitters had totally free access to the transmission channels and this led to purely random use of them. This situation was called 'pure' Aloha. It was possible for several units to transmit simultaneously to Menehune, thereby causing collision of packets which are corrupted on arrival at their destination. In this case, Menehune would clearly not send a reception acknowledgment and these packets must be retransmitted after a random delay for each station, with the risk of another collision. Because of the high probability of such events, the efficiency of the system was found to be low (at best 18.4 percent of the available passband). Attempts were therefore made to improve it and this led to a change to a slotted Aloha system in which the transmission periods are not left entirely at the liberty of the transmitters. The timescale is divided into segments whose duration corresponds to that required for the complete transmission of a packet (it is assumed that all packets are of the same length). A clock synchronizes the set by indicating to each transmitter the instant when it must start to transmit so that, taking account of the propagation delay, the start of every packet arrives at the central processor at the start of a segment. By means of this technique, the network efficiency was doubled to 36.8 percent of the available passband in the optimal case. Notice that later developments, based particularly on the reservation of transmission intervals, have permitted a significant increase in the system performance.

Another procedure frequently employed to limit the risk of collisions requires the station wishing to transmit to listen to check that there are no transmissions in progress before starting to send its data. This method is called *carrier sense multiple access* (CSMA) and was proposed in 1971 by Wax at the University of Hawaii. One variant that follows immediately is the CSMA/CD, where CD signifies *collision detection*.

While it is transmitting, the station continues to listen to the transmission medium; if it hears only its own message, all is well, otherwise there is interference and hence a collision. In this case, the station interrupts its transmission and resumes it after a random delay that is characteristic of it, as for the Aloha system. Using this procedure for collision detection, the use of time-consuming reception acknowledgments is avoided. It is, however, at present necessary to fix a lower limit for the length of messages; each must last twice as long as the time necessary for propagation to the most distant station otherwise some collisions may not be detected before the end of the transmission. The reader will have realized that the CSMA technique just described is very similar to the pure Aloha system. As for that system, other versions have been put into operation in a constant attempt to increase the efficiency of the procedures; in fact the one that has just been described corresponds to an *unslotted non-permanent* CSMA. Following the example of the Aloha system, the timescale can be divided into segments whose length is equal to the propagation time of a packet; each transmission must start at the beginning of a segment. This leads to a *slotted non-permanent* CSMA. The performance can be again increased by the use of *slotted p-permanent* CSMA. Here, the terminal listens to the transmission medium and, if it is free, it transmits its packet with probability p (it delays the transmission with probability $1 - p$). If the packet has not been transmitted, the process is repeated at the start of the following segment. If the transmission channel is busy, the terminal waits until it becomes free and proceeds as described previously. Protocols with segment reservation can also be used.

In the case of a cabled network, each station is capable of listening to the others and nothing prevents the use of a CSMA(/CD) procedure. Unfortunately, when terrestrial or satellite radio links are used, this can become impossible. For a network containing a central communication processor, the problem can be avoided by using the *busy tone multiple access* (BTMA) method in which the central station, when it receives a message, sends a 'busy' signal to all terminals.

Other methods for avoiding collisions will be described in Chapter 8 in the context of *local area networks*.

Several facilities relating to packet switching will now be considered; they are illustrated in Figure 7.1 and consist principally of the following:

- Confirmation (optional) of delivery of the message – verification that the latter has left the network by the interface to which the destination is connected.

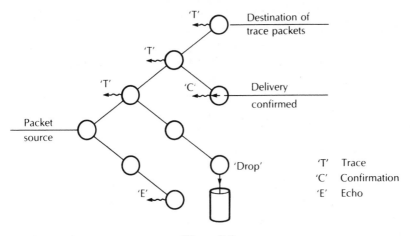

Figure 7.1

- Trace packets – in the case of a network which processes packets individually on an adaptive routing basis, it can be useful to know the path followed. This is the purpose of these packets; at each node which they visit, they send a report of their location to the transmitter until their arrival at the destination.
- 'Echo' – allows the procedures to be tested under realistic conditions by providing a special destination which returns the received packets to their despatcher after exchanging the origin and destination addresses.
- 'Drop' – a special destination which, unlike previous cases, discards received packets.

The principal standards established by the CCITT for packet switching networks will now be considered. The most important of these is without doubt the X.25 standard, which is devoted to virtual circuits and has already been mentioned in Chapter 5; recall that it covers the three lower layers of the OSI standard of the ISO.

At level 3 (the network level or packet level), 15 groups of logical channels are provided and each group contains 255 channels. It is at this stage that virtual circuit management is performed whether permanent or not. The frames for a command packet and a data packet are shown in Figures 7.2 and 7.3, respectively. It is immediately evident that the structure of these packets, whether for command or data transfer, is very similar.

The first two bytes are common to the two types and serve to control the logical channel; they contain the group and logical channel numbers

Figure 7.2

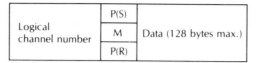

Figure 7.3

mentioned previously, together with information on packet sequence numbering. This is, in principle, performed modulo 8 but modulo 128 numbering can also be used. Use of a higher base number is justified by the fact that the window width, which determines the number of messages that can be transmitted before reception of an acknowledgment, must be less than this number. In the case of very long links, and because of the higher propagation delays, modulo 8 numbering could be a disadvantage.

The significance of the third byte differs between command packets and data transfer packets. In the latter case, the least significant bit (bit 0) of the byte has the value 0; the byte also contains two 3-bit counters (bits 1–3 and 5–7) and one *more* bit (bit 4). In the case of modulo 128 numbering, two bytes are used and the counters are of 7 bits. Although Standard X.25 recommends, in principle, a maximum of 128 bytes for the field reserved for data, all powers of 2 between 16 and 1024 are permissible. In the case of *virtual calls*, the size of the packets can be established independently for each extremity of the virtual circuit. The *more* bit serves to define a sequence of packets (consecutive packets with this bit at 1 and a packet with this bit at 0), for example, to indicate the limits of a packet which has been divided in order to conform to the specification of a destination for which the maximum authorized length is less than that of the transmitter. This bit can also be used to authorize recombination of packets into a single one, which can be useful when the length permitted by the destination is greater than that of the transmitted packet. In this way the number of delivered packets is reduced and the utilization coefficient of the receiver buffers is improved. The two counters give the transmitted packet number and the number of the next packet to be received, respectively. In addition to the information already mentioned, the most significant bit of the first byte can serve to distinguish two data levels when there are two destination processes – an intermediate one and a final one. For one level, the data will be transparent for the intermediate process and not for the other. When only a single level is possible, this bit has the value 0.

The commands defined by the contents of the third byte and possibly specified further in the subsequent ones will now be considered. In outline, the essential commands are as follows:

Call
(Confirmation of) clearing
(Confirmation of) interrupt
Receiver (Not) Ready
(Confirmation of) reset
(Confirmation of) restart
Reject.

Some of these commands, together with the packet numbering mechanism, can give the illusion of being very similar to the HDLC mechanisms and interchangeable with them. This is not the case; the level 3 procedures serve to control the flow of packets while those of level 2 have the object of avoiding transmission errors. The *reset* operation clears the logical channel of all data packets and reinitializes packet flow control. A *restart* action interrupts all the *virtual calls* and causes *reset* of all the *permanent virtual circuits* associated with a particular DTE. The 'Receiver Not Ready' command is used by the data terminal equipment (DTE) or the data communication equipment (DCE) to signal that it cannot accept data packets on a logical channel. This condition is lifted by transmission of a 'Receiver Ready' packet. The *reject* command enables the DTE to request the DCE to retransmit packets from a certain number.

The operation of a *virtual call* will now be considered from establishment of communication to its termination; the whole procedure is represented in Figure 7.4. The calling DTE sends a 'CALL REQUEST' packet to the DCE that is connected to it, preferably on the free logical channel of highest number among those that are allocated to it by the network management. The DCE transmits an 'Incoming Call' packet to the called DTE, preferably using the free logical channel on the interface having the lowest number. At this stage, two possibilities arise: either the called terminal refuses the communication and initiates a clearing procedure, to be discussed later, or it accepts the call by sending a 'Call Accepted' packet to the network, which in turn transmits a 'Call Connected' packet to the calling equipment and data transfer starts. The clearing procedure can be initiated on the initiative of one or other of the two terminal equipments by sending a 'Clear Request'

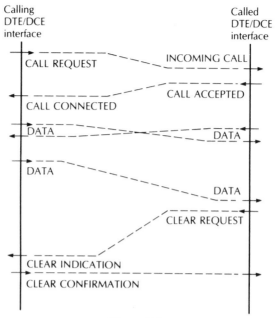

Figure 7.4

packet to the network, which transmits a 'Clear Indication' packet to the other DTE. In reply, a 'Clear Confirmation' packet is dispatched to request confirmation that clearing has been effected.

Recall that in the case of *permanent virtual circuits*, the parties establishing and clearing the communication do not exist at level 3; they are concerned directly with data transfer, as long as the lower levels (1 and 2) are active.

Consider level 2 (the *data link level*) of the X.25 standard, which is situated immediately below that which has just been described. It is here that error detection is performed. It is fundamental to make clear the distinction between the role of this level and that of level 3, which is intended for flow control and information routing. The ISO High Level Data Link Control (HDLC) protocol is used for the data link layer. When packets from the immediately higher level (level 3) must be transmitted, this is done by means of I(nformation) format frames. The attention of the reader is again drawn to the fact that use of a Receiver Not Ready (RNR) frame at level 2 provides an additional facility for flow control, but this must be used with many precautions.

To complete the overview of the various layers of the X.25 standard, level 1 (the physical level) remains to be examined; this corresponds to the lowest layer of the OSI standard and relates to physical connections to the network. This physical layer is defined, when the user has direct access to a digital communication network, by the CCITT X.21 interface, which operates using eight exchange circuits whose functions are defined in standard X.24 and electrical characteristics in standards X.26 and X.27. When the user has the use of a public switched digital network which is accessible in an analog manner, an extension of the X.21 standard, the X.21 bis specification, is used and this is compatible with recommendation V.24. In contrast, when access is at a node or a packet switching network concentrator using a specialized analog circuit, specification V.24 is used. The list of the eight exchange circuits in the X.21 interface is given in Table 7.1. Circuit S provides timing information at the bit level, while circuit B, which is not always present, provides it at the byte level. Negative logic is used by this interface: a 1 corresponds to the low level (off) and a 0 to the high level (on). A communication timing diagram is given in Figure 7.5 in which SYN represents a synchronization character and IA5 represents characters of the CCITT International Alphabet no. 5 or the 7-bit ISO code.

Table 7.1

Circuit	Name	DTE	DCE
G	Signal ground		
Ga	DTE common return	●	
T	Transmission	●	
R	Reception		●
C	Control	●	
I	Indication		●
S	Signal element timing		●
B	Byte level timing		●

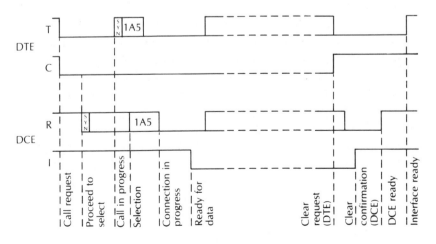

Figure 7.5

The various types of terminal and their method of connection to a packet switching network will now be considered. This data terminal equipment (DTE) can be classified into two groups. These consist of those which operate in 'character' mode (asynchronous, maximum capacity 1,200 baud) for which intermediate equipment for assembling and disassembling the packets is necessary (*packet assembler/disassembler* (PAD)) and those which operate in 'packet' mode (synchronous, capacity greater than 2,400 baud) for which clearly no PAD is required. The CCITT has specified three standards relating to PADs on public packet switching networks: the X.3 standard, which defines the facilities that a PAD must contain to process information to or from terminals of the 'character' or *start–stop* type (teletypes and their equivalents); the X.28 standard, which defines the interaction between the terminal and the PAD; and finally the X.29 standard, which treats the exchange of information between a terminal of the packet type and a PAD by way of a public packet switching network to which both are connected via an X.25 interface.

The essential functions that a PAD must fulfil, which are included in recommendation X.3, are as follows:

- Assembly of characters into packets; disassembly of packet data fields into characters.
- Establishment, interruption, reset and suppression of virtual calls.
- Generation of service signals for 'character' terminals.
- Sending of packets at the appropriate moment (for example, when the buffer is full and a predetermined delay has expired).
- Transmission of characters with start and stop elements to character terminals.
- Monitoring and interpretation of interrupt and break signals from character terminals.

The PAD can operate according to two standard profiles (transparent and simple) as determined by the values of certain parameters that can be read, modified and initialized by one or other of the communicating DTEs according to the procedures detailed in specifications X.28 and X.29. The list of these is given in Table 7.2.

The significance of these parameters will now be briefly explained:

1. This parameter, when its value is 1, permits the DTE to send command characters to the PAD instead of the other DTE; this facility is inhibited when this parameter has the value 0.
2. This parameter, when its value is 1, enables characters to be echoed to the terminal (to permit error detection); this facility is suppressed for a 0 value of the parameter.

Table 7.2

Parameter	Description	Transparent profile	Simple profile
1	PAD recall	No	Yes
2	Echo	No	No
3	Data forwarding	No	Note 1
4	Idle timer	1 s	Any
5	DTE flow control	No	Yes
6	Service signals	No	Yes
7	Action on break	Reset VC	Reset VC
8	Discard output	No	No
9	PAD after CR	No	No
10	Line folding	No	No
11	Binary speed	Note 2	Note 2
12	PAD flow control	No	Yes

Notes

1. The data are sent to the receiver for every IA5 control character or a 'DELete'.
2. Rates of 110,200 and 300 bits^{-1} are detected.

3. If this parameter has the value 2, packets, even if partially filled, are sent to the receiver on a carriage return; for a value of 126, they are sent to the receiver on an IA5 command character or a *delete*; for the value 0, no character is used.

4. Partially filled packets can be sent after listening for a certain delay; this parameter determines this delay in twentieths of a second (its value must be between 0 and 255).

5. This parameter, when it has the value 1, enables control of peripherals using DC1 (X-ON) and DC3 (X-OFF) of the IA5; this facility is suppressed when it has the value 0.

6. The service signals of the PAD are suppressed for a value 0 of this parameter and enabled for a value 1.

7. This parameter defines the behaviour of the PAD on reception of a *break* character: 0, no action; 1, interruption of virtual call; 2, virtual call reset; 4, send *break* to a packet terminal; 8, exit data transfer state; 16, ignore output of character terminals; and 21, combination of 16, 4 and 1.

8. The contents of the data field of the packets waiting to be delivered are not considered at the receiver on a *break* when this parameter has the value 1; if it has the value 0, delivery is performed normally.

9. This parameter permits automatic insertion, by the PAD, of 0–7 null characters after a carriage return command in order to provide time for physical execution.

10. This parameter permits a logical line to be divided automatically into several physical lines of appropriate length, by defining the length of a physical line (from 1 to 255 characters); when it has the value 0, this facility is suppressed.

11. This parameter indicates the speed of operation of 'character' terminals; 0, 110 bits^{-1}; 1, 134.5 bits^{-1}; 2, 300 bits^{-1}; 8, 200 bits^{-1}; 9, 100 bits^{-1} and 10, 50 bits^{-1}.

12. This parameter, when it has the value 1, enables character flow control between the PAD and a 'character' terminal by using X-ON and X-OFF signals (cf. parameter 5); for a value 0, this facility does not exist.

Recommendation X.28 defines the interface and protocols between a character terminal and the PAD to which it is connected; it contains four sections.

Section 1 treats the connection between the terminal and the PAD; this can be achieved by way of the telephone network (switched or leased lines) and modems, according to standard V.21, or by the use of public data transmission networks (switched or leased circuits) using X.20 and X.20 bis (V.21 compatible) interfaces when access to these is made by the telephone network.

Section 2 provides the format to be used for exchanged characters; a 7-bit code is used with one parity bit which is ignored by the PAD on input. The PAD itself generates characters with even parity. This section also describes the procedures for initialization, connection establishment and disconnection.

Section 3 covers the exchange of commands between the PAD and the terminal; this includes profile selection, modification of parameter values, request for connection establishment to a packet terminal and disconnection request.

Section 4 defines the exchange of the user's data between the PAD and the terminal (flow control and so on).

Recommendation X.29 is itself a kind of protocol established by the CCITT; it shows a variety of uses for the facilities provided by the X.25 specification, but more space will not be devoted to it.

It should be noted that various points of the X.25 standard remain to be examined. Among these are the following:

• The use of a *network user identifier* (NUI).
• The possibility of a packet terminal establishing a virtual call with a character terminal.
• The use of a character terminal in a mode other than *start–stop*.

Chapter 8

Public and local networks using packet communication

8.1 Public networks

In the United States, the principal networks of this type are Telenet and Tymnet.

Among European countries, Transpac in France and DCS in Belgium may be cited; the latter permits access to computers and databanks of the Canadian networks and the American Telenet and Tymnet networks.

The European Economic Community is also developing a network that links most of its member countries: Euronet permits access to computers and databanks of the Diane server. Among the databases accessible in this way are those of Télésystèmes-Questel, Infoline and the European Space Agency (ESA). Figure 8.1 shows a diagram of the network in its initial phase.

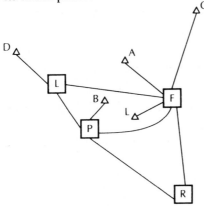

Figure 8.1

As illustrated, Euronet has four switching nodes at London, Paris, Frankfurt and Rome, together with five remote concentrators at Dublin, Amsterdam, Copenhagen, Brussels, and Luxembourg. Initially, only a system of virtual circuits which delivers packets in their order of transmission is provided; a datagram service will be added later. The performance required of this network is a *mean time between failures* (MTBF) of 200 h and a mean response time of 1–3 s (excluding processing time at the host station). The Euronet network will be connected to various other public data transmission networks including Transpac in France, the Experimental Packet Switching Service (EPSS) in Great Britain and the switched circuit public data transmission networks of the Federal Republic of Germany, and Denmark.

8.2 Local area networks (LANs)

8.2.1 General comments

As its name indicates, the object of this type of network is to permit interconnection of equipment within a limited geographical area over distances of a few kilometers at maximum. The most frequently used topologies are a bus in the form of a ring or a star; the links between equipment are realized directly using coaxial cables, twisted pairs of wires or even optical fibers.

These networks can be separated into two categories:

- *Closed networks*, which permit connection of equipment from a single manufacturer.
- *Open networks*, which provide the possibility of interconnecting equipment from diverse sources provided that there is a minimum specified compatibility, for example an exchange protocol.

It is clear, in view of the development of the OSI and IEEE-802 Standards, that it is the latter type of network that will be dominant in the future. The range of transmission speeds is rather extensive but extends, typically, from hundreds of kbaud to hundreds of Mbaud. The various types of local area network will now be reviewed.

8.2.2 Bus networks with the CSMA/CD access protocol

These bus networks use a random asynchronous access protocol, the *carrier sense multiple access/collision detection* (CSMA/CD), which was thoroughly examined in the previous chapter. It was the object of an attempt at standardization by way of the IEEE-802.3 Standard, which is itself compatible with the OSI specifications. Its principal disadvantage will be recalled – every increase in traffic inevitably causes an increase in the probability of collisions and an exponential increase in the waiting periods.

Among networks of this kind, one of the most widespread is the ETHERNET network, which was presented at the end of 1979 and is the result of cooperation between Xerox, Intel and Digital Equipment. It permits interconnection of 128 computers and terminals with a theoretical transmission speed of 10 Mbaud. Each local area network and each piece of equipment has its own address of 48 bits. In this way a destination recognizes that a message is intended for it. After an appropriate interval, the destination transmits a reception acknowledgment to the dispatcher. Equipment is connected to the network by means of a 50-coaxial cable.

The format of a packet is as follows:

- A preamble of 64 bits for synchronization and as a marker.
- The address of the destination.
- The address of the dispatcher.
- A field defining the protocol and format.
- The data field.
- The 32-bit CRC.

The minimum spacing between packets corresponds to 48 times the duration of 1 bit.

8.2.3 Bus and ring networks with a 'token' access protocol

These networks are also the object of a standardization attempt through specifications IEEE-802.4 (bus) and IEEE-802.5 (ring). They use a controlled asynchronous access protocol; the control is symbolized by a 'token' issued by a central station and circulated from one piece of equipment to another.

No station may transmit unless it is in possession of a 'free' token. The station then modifies the state of the token, which becomes 'occupied', and attaches its message to it, preceded by the address of the destination. This block is regenerated at each station on the route. At the destination, an address recognition indicator is added and the information is copied while the regeneration process operates. If the copy is made correctly, a correct copy indicator is added and the block returns to the transmitter, which withdraws its message and puts a 'free' token into circulation. In the case of a problem, the transmitting station is notified and takes appropriate measures when it again has access to a 'free' token. In the case where the station does not have a message to be transmitted, it can pass the token to its neighbor either immediately or after saving it for a time according to the protocol in operation. In ring structures, a hierarchy within the equipment can also be instituted with the possibility of reserving a token.

In the case of a ring network, the token frequently consists simply of an indicator having the value 0 or 1. In principle, it is necessary that the circulation time of the token should be longer than the duration of messages.

The principal advantage of the method resides in the fact that, because of the access philosophy and process, all risk of collision is eliminated. It is also possible to determine the maximum access time that arises when a station wishes to transmit although it has just passed the token. The mean access time is approximately half this value. For very long bus structures, it must be emphasized that delays in transferring the token form a potential problem.

By way of example, the IBM Token Ring Network and its facilities will be considered. This network, anounced by IBM at the beginning of October 1985, forms, as its name implies, a token ring from the logical point of view, although its physical topology is a star. It is possible to connect up to 260 workstations of the PC type by means of a plug-in adaptor card and cable; the transmission speed is of the order of 4 Mbaud. One of the basic elements of the network consists of the IBM 8228 *Multi-Station Access Unit*, which is a type of concentrator able to support up to eight stations. It is possible to extend the network in a modular manner according to the needs of the user. IBM has also developed interfaces that permit this network to be connected to others and to large central processing units. In particular, a PC connected to a ring network can access a host computer via an SDLC link. This PC is then considered by the host to be a monitor and the other PCs can operate autonomously or as terminals.

Chapter 9

Security of communication in networks

9.1 General considerations

For the benefit of users, it is generally necessary to guarantee, on the one hand, that no one has been able to obtain knowledge of the information during its transit through the network (secrecy of transmission), and, on the other hand, that the information received does originate from the assumed dispatcher and, in particular, has not been subjected to any possible modification during transmission (authenticity of information). The first of these aspects is particularly important in the case of the use of leased circuits; since the data follows a fixed route, it is very easily hijacked.

Secrecy of transmission is ensured by encoding on transmission and decoding on reception; these two operations are the inverse of each other. This procedure also has the effect of ensuring the authenticity of the received information in the majority of cases. Notice, however, that it is perfectly possible to ensure the authenticity of the delivered message without necessarily encoding it.

Conserving the secrecy of information and guaranteeing its authenticity are not problems that arise from the use of data processing. They arose in the military domain a long time ago. Numerous codes have been conceived and the application of very powerful mathematical theories for several decades have made them more and more powerful.

9.2 A standard for encoding data

The method of encoding and decoding must be sufficiently robust so that, even if the algorithm is known or fragments of the message have been decoded, it remains secure. Realization of these objectives necessitates the use of a key which, if it is identical at the two extremities, guarantees deciphering of the encrypted message. Finally, the most crucial part resides in the transmission of the key, which must be achieved using a secure method. It is partly on account of the sensitivity of this that a distinction is made between conventional encoding systems and the *public key system*.

One of the best procedures published to date is undoubtedly the Data Encryption Standard (DES). It presently forms the United States Federal Information Processing Standard, which must be used for transmission of data for government use which is not classified but requires secret transmission.

The block diagram of a device to provide coding and decoding of messages and the generation of keys is shown in Figure 9.1. In order to take account of the preceding design features, a parallel input and output are available that can accept a byte of encoded text, uncoded text or text serving as the key. The last is saved in an internal register and can never be read from the exterior. This register is loaded from the input or from the contents of the output register. The key can, therefore, be entered into the system in a coded form, based on the value of the key present at that moment.

The bytes from the input are placed end to end, in groups of eight, in a shift register. The coding mechanism contains two distinct parts. One consists of generating 16 different sub-keys. This is done from 64 bits

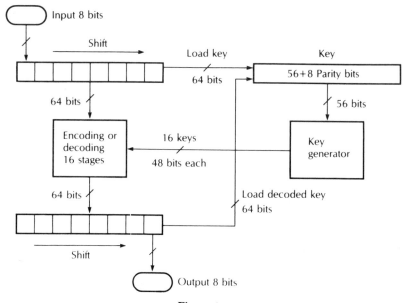

Figure 9.1

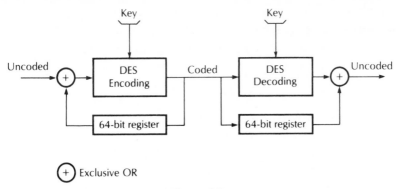

Figure 9.2

contained in the shift register; they are subdivided into one key of 56 bits with 8 bits of parity and, from this, 16 sub-keys each of 48 bits are formed. The other part consists of encoding the data. This operation is performed in sixteen logical steps, each of which makes use of one of the 16 sub-keys previously generated. Decoding uses the same procedure as coding but with the sub-keys generated in the inverse order.

Coding obtained in the manner just described is, unfortunately, still not perfect. Repetitive grouping of uncoded text would also appear in the coded message and, by examining this, it would be possible to decode the message. Secret service code specialists are well aware of this danger. By way of example, it is possible to break the code by observing the frequency with which certain groups of characters recur and knowing the most used letters in the language employed.

One method of avoiding this disadvantage is to include a random or sequential number in the first block and to make the coding of each block dependent on the contents of the previous block. This principle is illustrated in Figure 9.2. Before initiating coding, the contents of the previously coded block are added, modulo 2, to the block to be coded. At the receiver, the coded message is stored and added to the following message after decoding.

9.3 Message authentification

9.3.1 General considerations

To know whether a message is authentic or not, it is necessary to return to its origin and this often requires the system to identify the person using the terminal. It must not be possible for an intruder to pass, in the eyes of the system, for someone having authorization for access or a transaction. It must, however, be humbly recognized that no system can be made perfectly secure; there is always a flaw and the aim is to make the task as complicated as possible for would-be pirates. The three methods of identification currently used will now be reviewed.

9.3.2 Knowledge-based identification

This consists of the use of a *personal identification number* (PIN) or the well known *password* formed from a certain number of alphanumeric characters. The user contributes, to a large extent, to the security aspect by keeping his password secret. He must neither divulge it inadvertently nor write it anywhere; he must also take care that no one unexpectedly sees the characters typed when it is entered. It is also crucial not to choose a password that is easy to discover because of its mnemonic aspects (date of birth, forename and so on). At the data processing level, it is vital to protect the list of users and their corresponding passwords against any fraudulent attempt to read them.

9.3.3 Identification based on a physical key

In this method, use is made of badges, magnetic cards and other similar devices. Here also, the user is partly responsible for security; he must not leave his card around inconsiderately and must take care not to lose it and so on. If possible, the device should also be realized in such a way that making a copy is not simple.

9.3.4 Identification based on personal characteristics of the user

This method is based on recognition of a characteristic peculiar to the user (voice, fingerprint, signature and so on). One of the main problems with this procedure is to provide a compromise between allowing access to a person who is not authorized and rejecting access to a person who is. Curves representing these two possibilities are given in Figure 9.3. To avoid incorrect refusal of use of the system to a user having the right of access, several chances are generally given to the person presenting himself.

9.3.5 Authentification of uncoded messages

It has been noted previously that, as a general rule, the use of cryptography allows a guarantee that the contents of a message have not been changed during transmission. In the case where cryptography is

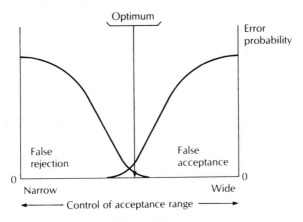

Figure 9.3

not used, in other words the text is sent without coding, authenticity of the message can be ensured by adding additional information to it which depends on the data block and a secret key. At the receiver, this information is recalculated and, if it proves to be identical to that received, authenticity is proved.

9.4 Coding system using a public key

The fundamental distinction between this procedure and the DES resides in the fact that here, contrary to the case with the DES, the keys used by the transmitter and the receiver are different; the encoding and decoding algorithms themselves can be similar or different. Figure 9.4 shows the functional block diagram of the encoding and decoding system.

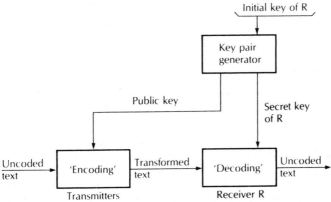

Figure 9.4

The reader will immediately notice that the two keys actually used (one public and one secret) are not totally independent but are both derived from a single initial key at the receiver. The essential advantage of this method consists of the fact that the encoding key is public. The encoding and decoding functions must evidently be inverses of each other when the public key–private key pair is correct. It is also necessary that the public key should be a function of the secret key whose inverse cannot be calculated; the same must apply to the coded text with respect to the uncoded text.

A similar arrangement also permits authenticity of messages to be ensured, as illustrated in Figure 9.5. For this purpose, it is assumed that the uncoded and coded messages have the same number of bits. It is also assumed that the encoding algorithm causes an equal number of possibilities for the coded text to correspond to all possible cases of the uncoded message and that the decoding function ensures the inverse correspondence; there is therefore bijection between uncoded and coded text. The encoding and decoding stages are 'permuted' in such a way that the public and secret keys are now generated at the transmitter. In Figure 9.5, encoding and decoding are denoted in order to indicate the purpose served. In reality the decoding and encoding mechanisms are the same as those used for encoding and decoding respectively in Figure 9.4.

It is perfectly possible to combine encoding of messages to ensure secrecy and verification of their authenticity by using the procedures described in cascade, as shown in Figure 9.6.

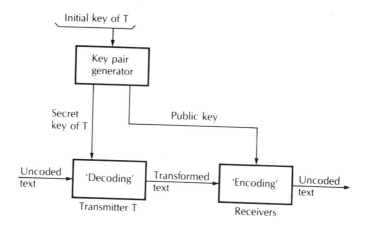

Figure 9.5

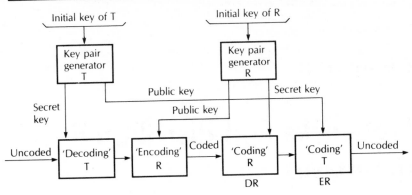

Figure 9.6

Chapter 10

Networks and distributed databases

10.1 Introduction

By using communication networks, it is possible to have access not only to 'conventional' databases where the information is centralized (stored in one fixed place) but also to databases in which the information is stored, in a distributed manner, at various nodes of the network, thereby forming a single, globally coherent entity.

10.2 Advantages and restrictions of distributed databases

By using a distributed structure, the aim is to achieve the following goals:

- More rapid responses to questions from users.
- Reduction of costs associated with data transmission by reduced use of the communication network.
- Uniformity of logical access on the part of all stations.
- Sharing of data between nodes situated at geographically distinct locations.
- Distribution and storage of information at nodes that have very high utilization rates.
- Increased reliability by ensuring continuity of service even in the case of loss of one or more nodes.
- The possibility of extending the size of the database at existing nodes or by the addition of new nodes.

Among the objectives cited previously, a number can be realized by making use of the redundancy of information. In spite of such an approach, the problem of data integrity does not completely disappear; in contrast, it is increased. It is therefore necessary to ensure the following functions, as in the case of a centralized system:

- The information must be capable of automatic restoration in case of error or even a serious fault.
- The data must be capable of protection against illegal access by unauthorized persons, and it must therefore be possible to assign access 'privileges'.
- The resources must be used in an optimum manner by the use of appropriate algorithms.
- In the case of multiple copies of data, it must remain coherent without causing unacceptable delays in operation.
- All stations must have an equal priority.
- It must not be possible for any transaction to be blocked following an attempt to use an unavailable resource (the phenomenon of *deadlock*).

10.3 Implementation

Firstly, some fundamental concepts concerning centralized databases will be reviewed; these concepts remain applicable in the case of distributed systems.

From the data modeling point of view, the two most developed approaches at the present time are as follows:

- *The network approach.* Data records which have common characteristics are grouped together; the user is obliged to specify in detail the storage structures, the data structures and the access routes that actually represent the interrelationships between the properties of the various groups of data. The fact that paths which are not specified initially can never be used makes this type of database rather inflexible. The special case of the hierarchical network model where each 'member' group belongs, and is linked, only to a single 'proprietor' is mentioned again.
- *The relational approach.* Information is stored in the form of 'relations' which form a table where each line forms a record or tuple, and each column forms a component. Prior specification of access paths is not obligatory in order to improve performance.

Among the various components of a database, a typical system includes:

- Application software.

- An operating system that forms the interface between the user's application and the data management system and controls all mass memories.
- Physical allocation of storage.
- Data management software.
- The data.
- The data format definition at system level (the schema).
- The data format definition at user level (the sub-schema).

In the context of a distributed base, those elements closely related to data are located at system nodes; this immediately raises the problem of choosing the distribution of the application software, data management, the data and their definitions. The result is a large number of possible combinations. When the data are stored at several nodes, their definitions must be adapted to a situation of this kind and their management software must be capable of accessing and processing them as if they were centralized. When a user request and the data are situated at different nodes, it is necessary for the data management functions to be distributed also. It is also fundamental to provide, throughout the network, a definition of the location and characteristics of all the data in the system; this information forms a kind of *directory*. When the system receives a request from a user, it must first determine whether or not the data are situated at the same node as the user. If the data are not accessible locally, it is necessary to determine the appropriate node and initiate communication with it. In this situation, there may not be direct compatibility between the nodes and therefore conversion functions must be used to ensure compatibility.

With respect to a centralized system, a distributed database must have the following two additional components:

- A *directory*, network-wide, of all the data contained in the system. This contains the logical information which relates the various data units to the nodes where they reside.

- A data management system, at network level, which must be capable of taking into account all aspects relating to the geographical distribution of the data. This includes: interception of the question and determination of the location of the data; access to the data directory and sending the question to the node that has the data if this is not local; coordination of all responses and processing when several nodes are used in the course of an access; constitution of the interface between the user and the local and remote data management systems together with the various directories within the system; possible conversion of commands and data in the case of a heterogeneous environment.

Distribution of data across the network can be performed in two ways:

- The data may be partitioned by associating the data that it calls most frequently with each node, thereby maximizing local access. In the case where the application is such that all data accesses are realized locally, the data are said to be segmented into disjoint sets.
- Several copies of the same data may be used within the system (in the limit, one copy per node); this considerably improves performance, reliability and costs but greatly complicates the problem of coherence of information, particularly during updating.

As a general rule, when the volume of data is small, the use of multiple copies is justified except when the frequency of updating is high. In this case it is better, as long as the local access rate remains high, to use data partitioning, otherwise a centralized database is more appropriate. If the amount of data is large, the best solution lies in partitioning, except when updates are numerous and the local access rate is low, in which case a centralized system is more convenient. It is possible to use a combination of the two techniques; for example, two copies of the entire database at two nodes with partitioning of data between the other nodes of the system. In this way an attempt can be made to adapt the distribution of data to the needs of users at different nodes.

All the considerations developed for data apply equally to the directory, which can also be subject to multiple copies and/or partitioning or could be centralized. Processing is therefore exactly similar to that to which the data is subjected.

In view of the advantages inherent in the use of multiple copies, numerous studies relating to updating of data have been made. The result is that the problems related to guaranteeing the integrity of data are extremely complex when updates must be made 'on line' as is the case, for example, with reservations for aircraft seats, hotel rooms and so on. In principle, each node is in process of updating only after an unknown and unpredictable delay. Consequently, the solution consists of strict control of this delay with the penalty of destruction of the integrity of the data. In centralized systems or without redundancy of information, this is achieved by setting interlocks that authorize updates only one after the other, in a serial manner. In the case of multiple copies, it is also necessary for the updates to be applied to all copies and always in the same order. It is clear that it is highly desirable to have the set of copies updated at the same time, that is to have 'high integrity'. Unfortunately, updating delays increase the response time and it is necessary to be content with a 'low integrity' in order to be able to make better use of resources; the copies converge to the same state but, at each instant, they differ from each other in respect of the number of updates already performed. The system designer must therefore opt for one and/or the other solution according to the application to be realized.

To prevent any blocking of a transaction that wishes to use an unavailable resource (the phenomenon of *deadlock*), the same techniques as those used in multiprogramming systems can be used; they consist of the following:

- Prevention. To do this, it is necessary to know, at the start, all the resources to be used in such a way as to be able to reserve them at the beginning of the transaction. Such knowledge is very often impossible to obtain in practice since the use of resources is a function of the data; in addition, this method causes under-use of available facilities.
- Avoidance. This technique is very similar to prevention but prior knowledge of the resources which will be used is more limited; however, it has disadvantages similar to those of prevention.
- Detection. This method is based on searching for cycles in a state diagram of the utilization of resources; this enables the risks of deadlock to be deduced.

Good performance, as noted previously, is related to the use of well-chosen algorithms. By way of example, if a question calls for data situated at different nodes, it is better if the communication costs dominate those associated with interpretation of a complex question. The latter is decomposed into elementary parts that call for local data and transfer this within elementary local questions; this is preferable to bringing all of the data required for treatment of the original question to a single node.

Restoration methods, in the case of a failure, resemble those used in the context of centralized databases but are more complex to realize. They vary according to whether or not there is redundancy as follows:

- Data partitioned without redundancy. In the case of failure, all transactions are interrupted and the system attempts to return to the state that it has just left. If this does not succeed, it returns to the last state saved and arrives at the point where operations were interrupted by making use of the 'diary' where successive modifications are recorded.

- Multiple copies. On this assumption, the system continues to operate except for the node or link that is out of use; when the unavailable element becomes operational again, if the interruption has been brief, the updates that are missing from the 'diary' are performed from another node. For a prolonged period out of service, it is preferable to recopy all the data initially from a neighboring node that contains them and then to perform the latest updates.

10.4 Conclusion

Distributed databases and the problems that they pose form an area where research is particularly active. In the majority of cases, satisfactory solutions have already been proposed, which augurs well for their future development in the next decade, particularly as hardware costs decrease and communication network performance improves continuously. They will contribute without doubt, in the near future, to an improvement of and an increase in the services offered to users.

Chapter 11

Network optimization

11.1 Introduction

The essential goal of optimization is to make the 'best use' of the diverse available network components such as switching nodes, concentrators, multiplexers and transmission lines, while taking account of their respective performance and the possible constraints that bear on the arrangement of the system. The meaning of 'best use' remains to be specified; in the great majority of cases it consists of finding the most economic solution to a certain criterion of performance. The problem posed here proves to be extremely complex and abundant literature has already been devoted to it. The following will be limited to an outline of the main lines of approach used.

As it is the size and dispersion that predominantly influence the cost and performance of a network, the first factor that affects optimization will be of a geographical nature and will, to a large extent, determine the location of the terminal equipment.

In view of the wide range of performance, a second very important factor is formed by the matrix that defines the required traffic capacities from one terminal point to all the others across the network. It is good practice for this evaluation to consider the mean hourly traffic at the busiest time of day.

A third factor to be taken into consideration relates to the available components, which have their own topological limitations, for example the maximum number of connections.

Most frequently, the problem of interconnecting equipment is resolved by proceeding in stages. The terminals and their connection to multiplexers and concentrators are considered first; this is followed by the principal switching nodes and finally by the communication lines joining the nodes.

As in the majority of problems that depend on the skill of the engineer, the optimum solution results from a compromise; it is, for example, impossible to minimize the cost of the network and the mean information transmission delay at the same time. This leads to optimization of a figure of merit that takes account of the compromise between the various parameters, or optimization of one of these while imposing constraints on the others.

The principal parameters concerned are the cost, to which optimization relates in the majority of cases and for which a single figure of merit for the scale of the network is sufficient, the capacity, the delay and the reliability. The capacity of the network is directly related to the matrix that defines the traffic volume to be supported between different points. Sometimes this capacity is not given but must be maximized; the matrix in question is then multiplied by a scaling factor, which is then optimized. The matrix now describes only the various proportions in which the traffic distributes itself within the network. The delay can be expressed in the form of a mean transit time for all traffic, but it is particularly useful to know its variations. In practice, the mean delay is often treated as the optimization criterion when it is desired to minimize this parameter; the probable distribution is then calculated and checked for acceptability. Reliability is measured as the percentage of time during which the network is available to all users. It depends strongly on the failure rates of the various equipment together with the mean repair time. A constraint that bears on the reliability can generally be considered from the point of view of a condition of the degree of interconnection in the network, that is as a topological constraint measured by the connectivity, which will be considered again later.

It should be noted that the manner in which the constraints are imposed differs between public and private data transmission networks. For private networks, the sites chosen for location of the nodes belong, in principle, to the organization, and it is the volume of traffic that will normally determine their location. The only level at which optimization can play an important role is that of the topology. In other words, how will the connections between equipment be organized? This problem, above all, is crucial during first installation of the network; subsequently, every modification of the constraints leads to a new, relatively small, optimization problem. In addition, the manner in which communication costs are taken into account in private networks is generally artificial since the tariffs considered do not represent the real costs. In contrast, for a public network, the equipment and the access points to the existing means of transmission form non-negligible constraints to the optimization; it would be preferable, for example, to install the nodes where several transmission lines already meet. In addition, contrary to the case of private networks, the costs taken into consideration correspond to real costs; it is also necessary to provide, on a large scale, future extensions about which little is known at the time of optimization of the network.

The techniques used will now be briefly introduced. Due notably to the progress made in operational research and linear, non-linear and combinational programming, mathematical tools that facilitate network optimization are starting to appear. These optimization problems can, in fact, be approached in a combinational, heuristic or analytic manner.

As its name indicates, in the combinational method an attempt is made to find all the possible relations from a finite set of elements; it is immediately evident that the number of possible combinations is very often extremely high, which makes this method very unproductive or even impossible to operate in view of the necessary calculation time. On the other hand, certain problems, for example the distribution of flow between the various transmission lines in such a way as to optimize the total capacity of the network, have an analytic solution. In practice, it is often necessary to make use of approximations to reduce the problem to a linear one. The justification underlying the approximations lies in the fact that the solution found is normally close to the real optimum. However, it is often preferable to make use of a heuristic, trial-and-error method based on successive improvements achieved by the application of more or less empirical rules. Random perturbations are introduced to guarantee that one of the *better solutions* is sufficiently close to the optimum. For a starting point, the best attempt from a series of random ones is chosen. In fact, when the problem is fundamentally analytical or combinational, the heuristic approach often proves to be the best.

11.2 Elements of graph theory

A graph is formed from a set of nodes connected together by *lines* or *edges*. If the connection contains a sense of direction or orientation, it is described as an *arc*. If there is no specified direction, the edge consists of two arcs oriented in opposite directions. A set of consecutive lines is called a *route* and a *cycle* when the points of departure and arrival are identical. The number of lines ending at or leaving a node forms the *degree* of that node.

The arcs between the nodes of a graph can be represented by the *adjacency matrix* of the graph; this matrix provides the number of arcs. It is illustrated in Figure 11.1.

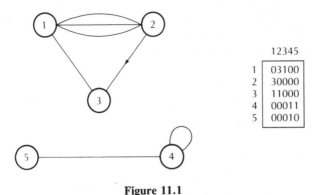

Figure 11.1

Notice the following:

- The adjacency matrix of the example is not symmetrical on account of the directional link between nodes 2 and 3; in networks, this does not normally exist and it can be assumed in practice that the adjacency matrix is symmetrical.
- Node 4 is linked to itself, which is of very little significance for the analysis of networks; consequently, the diagonal elements are considered to be zero.
- The graph of Figure 11.1 consists of two distinct parts; this condition does not exist in communication networks, except in the case of a fault.

The adjacency matrix has the following useful properties; raised to the pth power, it gives the number of routes formed from p edges between the various nodes.

If a network contains p nodes, they are all interconnected if the matrix formed by the sum:

$$I + A + A^2 + \ldots + A^{p-1}$$

where I is the identity matrix and A, the adjacency matrix, has no zero elements; satisfaction of this condition indicates, therefore, that the graph is connected.

When the dimension of the adjacency matrix is large and it is relatively sparse, that is many of its elements are zero, it is easier to test for connectivity by making use of a labeling algorithm rather than different powers of the adjacency matrix.

In this procedure, an initial node is chosen arbitrarily and all nodes that are connected to it are passed through by visiting them at least once. If it happens that all nodes of the graph are passed through in this way, it is formed only of a single part. The various lines can serve only twice, once in the outward direction and once in the return direction. Consequently, they are provided with a label that indicates the number of times that they have already been covered. The algorithm provides rules that permit determination of the line by which to leave the node which has just been reached. They will be examined by distinguishing between the outward phase (the first covering of the line) and the return phase (the second and last permitted covering of the line).

For the outward phase where the access line to the node has still only been used once, these rules are:

- If all the lines connected to the node, other than the line of arrival, still do not carry a label, the node is left by any of them and the phase remains outward; if the line of arrival is the only line connected to the node, it is left by this same line and the phase becomes return.
- If one or more lines connected to the node, other than that of arrival, carry a label, the node must be left by the access line and the phase becomes return.

In the return phase, the access line is used for the second time and cannot be used again; the rules to be applied are then as follows:

- If there is an unlabeled line connected to the node, the node is left by this route and returns to the outward phase.
- Otherwise, if there is a line that has not yet been used twice, it is used to leave the node.
- Otherwise, if all lines have been covered twice, the algorithm is terminated.

To check that the number of nodes visited is indeed equal to the number of nodes in the network, a counter is used which is incremented by one each time the first situation analyzed in the outward phase is encountered and its value, at the end of the procedure, is compared with the number of nodes in the graph.

The concept of connectivity has already been introduced without defining it; its meaning will now be specified. Connectivity allows a measure of the extent to which a network remains in a single piece in the case of loss of one or more nodes; more precisely, the connectivity of a network is equal to the minimum number of nodes that must fail for the network to cease to consist of a single part. A similar quantity relating to the minimum number of lines to be lost can also be defined; it is the cohesion.

Denoting the connectivity by n, the cohesion by l and the minimum degree of the graph by d, it can be shown that the following inequality is satisfied:

$$n \leqslant l \leqslant d$$

The fact that n is the lower bound of the preceding relation shows that a good measure of the reliability of the network is the connectivity rather than the cohesion.

Although the connectivity and the cohesion can be determined easily by inspection in the case of small networks, this is not so when the size increases. Determination of the connectivity can be based on the result of Whitney's theorem, which states that a network has a connectivity n if, among all the nodes taken two by two, there are n routes that do not contain any common nodes except, of course, the departure and arrival nodes. In a similar manner, the network has a cohesion l if, among all the nodes taken two by two, there are l routes that do not contain common lines. To apply these methods, systematic searching algorithms may be used within the network. For large networks, however, the volume of operations increases considerably if the techniques just described are used. Fortunately, exact knowledge of the connectivity is not often necessary; it is sufficient to establish that it reaches at least a given value. In this case, use can be made of the Kleitman test whose principle is as follows. Assume that it is required to check that the network has a connectivity equal to or less than n. A node N is chosen arbitrarily and examined for connection to each other node of the network by at least n routes without common nodes. Then, the node N is eliminated from the graph and the operation is repeated, based this time on $n-1$ routes. The procedure continues in this way until n nodes have been eliminated and then terminates by verifying that the remaining part of the graph is connected.

11.3 Availability of the network

This quality of the network can be quantified by making use of statistical quantities and assuming that the lines and nodes fail and are repaired in an independent manner. In this way an identical first probability of failure for all the lines and a similar second probability for all the nodes can be used. A global failure probability can then be evaluated and hence the unavailability of the network. This is performed by summing the probabilities that correspond to the various possible combinations of out of service elements.

It should be noted that a mesh structure is more resistant to the loss of lines than a star or tree structure.

11.4 Optimization of line capacity and traffic distribution

If it is assumed that the topology of the network is fixed, optimization relates to the capacities to be assigned to the various lines and the manner in which the traffic is distributed between them; in practice, the latter point results from algorithms that manage the routing of information. In the case where the aim is flow optimization, this leads to a better solution than in the case where more traditional methods of route determination are used; these consider neither the totality of the network nor its constraints in respect of the capacities of the various lines.

To resolve this problem, it is obligatory to have available the matrix that represents the maximum volumes of traffic, to ensure distribution between the various nodes, and a relation between the cost of a line and its capacity. The problem can be approached in two ways: either a constant total cost is specified and the mean delay between transmission of a message and its arrival at the destination is minimized; or a limit on the mean delay is specified and the total cost is minimized. In fact, the results achieved in practice are similar whichever route is chosen.

Generally, instead of searching immediately for the flows and line capacities that minimize the cost or delay, it is preferable to examine the problems of choice of capacities and flow distribution separately at first and to combine them later. In doing this a function is found that very often has several local optima; this clearly raises the problem of finding the global optimum. That is why it is customary to avoid the difficulty by performing several successive optimizations for which the initial flows are generated randomly; values are then chosen that lead to better local optima. This process is, of course, purely heuristic but it provides satisfactory results.

The first stage of optimization will now be examined, to research the capacities of the various lines on the assumption of a fixed data flow in each of them. The cost of the line depends on its length and its capacity. Normally, as the possible capacities (expressed in $bits^{-1}$ or b.p.s.) can take only well-defined values, the cost function is not known. However, it is conventional to assume a linear relation between capacity and cost; not using this assumption leads to results very far from the real values obtained without approximation. As the flows on a line cannot be identical in the two transmission directions, the line is divided into two channels that each correspond to one direction. Following the assumptions which have been introduced, a capacity C_i, to be determined, a cost $d_i C_i$, where d_i is a known factor, and a flow λ_i are associated with each channel i. Rigorous calculation of the mean delay T is rather complex;

consequently, to simplify the formulation, certain approximations will be introduced whose validity is not questioned in reality. Firstly, a mean delay T_i, which is the sum of the waiting and service times, is associated with each channel i. By introducing γ, the total traffic within the network, that is the number of packets entering (and hence leaving) per second, the relationship between T and the T_i is given by:

$$\gamma T = \sum_i \lambda_i T_i$$

The packet arrival intervals have a very complex distribution since the packets themselves generally consist of the outputs of other queues. The first to treat this problem in detail was Kleinrock who proposed an approach to the process as an $M/M/1$ system for which the packets arrive according to a Poisson process of rate λ_i and the service times are exponentially distributed with a mean $1/\mu C_i$. Using these approximations, the mean delay for each channel is obtained from the following equation:

$$T_i = 1/(\mu\, C_i - \lambda_i)$$

The expression for the mean global delay T then becomes:

$$T = \sum_i \lambda_i/\gamma\,(\mu\, C_i - \lambda_i)$$

By way of example, minimization of T with the constraint that the total cost does not exceed a certain value K will be considered. The following expression for the capacities is then obtained:

$$C_i = (\lambda_i/\mu) + k\sqrt{\lambda_i}$$

where k is a constant such that:

$$\sum_i d_i\, C_i \leq K$$

The first term of the relation that defines the capacities represents the minimum capacity that each channel must have, the capacity for which the queue would become infinite.

For a given line, the capacities of each of its channels are clearly identical in practice. This applies to the previous equations only for the case of a minimum flow matrix which is symmetrical; if not, it will generally be necessary to choose a value for the capacity of the line that is a compromise between the capacities of each of its channels.

The problem of choosing the best route for the information will now be considered. At this stage, the cost is no longer involved since it has been determined by the capacities selected at the previous stage. It is now required to minimize T by operating on the flows, that is the λ_i. In a given channel i, packets circulate from sources s with destinations d; the flow corresponding to a pair (s,d) will be denoted by $f(s,d,i)$ and considered to be positive. Hence:

$$\lambda_i = \sum_s \sum_d f(s,d,i)$$

Two types of constraint must be observed as follows:

• For each pair (s,d) and for each node N, the flow entering the node must be equal to that leaving it; mathematically, it is necessary that:

$$\alpha(N) - \beta(N) + \sum_{i \in v_1} f(s,d,i) - \sum_{i \in v_2} f(s,d,i) = 0$$

where v_1 and v_2 represent the sets of indices that correspond to the lines of arrival and departure respectively of node N; $\alpha(N)$ and $\beta(N)$ represent the number of packets per second entering and leaving the network at node N, respectively.
• The flow in each channel certainly cannot exceed the corresponding capacity:

$$\lambda_i \leq C_i$$

The problem is one of optimization in which the objective function T is not linear while the constraints are; furthermore it has a global optimum that guarantees that the solution found is optimal. It can be resolved by making use of iterative non-linear programming methods based, for example, on the use of gradients. There is much literature on this subject and the procedures considered emerge from this work.

Relatively large networks, that is those that contain at least twenty nodes and whose matrix elements representing the traffic to be supported are all of the same order of magnitude, form an interesting case. An algorithm that imposes a fixed route on the packets according to their source and destination, based on the optimum solution obtained, is particularly suitable since a modification of flow allocation, in principle, has only an infinitesimal effect on the value of the mean global delay T.

When it is required to examine the problem of optimization of capacities and flow distribution in a global manner, and hence to combine the two sub-problems that have been analyzed alone, conditions arise where it is necessary to minimize T by operating on the variables that constitute the capacities and flows, while observing the constraint of not exceeding a predetermined total cost. As the form of the relation between capacity and flow is known, this expression can be used to transform the problem into another that is equivalent to it and no longer depends only on the flows but which unfortunately has several local optima. To resolve this, the iterative optimization methods mentioned previously can be used. Furthermore, the operation can be repeated several times by choosing random points as the start for the iterative process. In this way it is hoped to reach different local optima so that the best of them can be chosen subsequently. This procedure, although entirely heuristic, has the advantage of providing good results in practice.

11.5 Optimization of topology

The first comment that must be made on this topic relates to the fact that it is not impossible, during the flow optimization stage, to obtain a solution for which the flow in a line is zero. In such a situation, the first task is clearly to eliminate the line in question from the network; for reasons of reliability its presence is not required.

Having made this statement, it must be admitted that optimization of the topology reduces very often to a process of trial and error based on exchanging lines or adding lines when links become saturated; clearly, only configurations that lead to performance improvement are retained. Nevertheless, the topologies envisaged must satisfy certain criteria that have already been stated. Briefly restated, these are to ensure a minimum degree of connectivity and to permit a sufficiently high throughput for a minimum mean global delay, or cost, according to the optimization criterion.

11.6 Conclusion

In view of the constant developments in linear, non-linear and combinational programming, together with the increasing calculating power of computers, it is not unreasonable to hope for the eventual appearance of methods with a reduced heuristic element or even the capability of processing the different possible combinations relating to network configurations in an exhaustive manner.

Bibliography

Commission des Communautés Européennes – Information scientifique et technique et gestion de l'information, Euronet: le réseau européen d'information 'on line'.

Commission des Communautés Européennes – Information scientifique et technique et gestion de l'information, Guide Euronet–Diane.

Davies, D. W., Barber, D. L. A., Price, W. L. and Solomonides, C. M. 1983. *Computer Networks and their Protocols*. John Wiley.

Deasington, R. 1984. *A Practical Guide to Computer Communications and Networking*. John Wiley.

Graube, M. 1982. Local area nets: a pair of standards, *IEEE Spectrum*, no. 6.

Healey, R. 1973. Computer network simulation study. National Physical Laboratory report COM-64.

IBM Informations. 1985. Communication et échanges d'informations? Les réseaux locaux, *IBM Informations*, no. 116 (Oct.–Dec.).

Intel handbooks.

International Standards Organization. *Data Link Control Procedures – Elements of Procedure (independent numbering)*, ISO/DIS4335.

International Standards Organization. *HDLC-classes of procedure*, ISO/TC97/SC6/N 1501.

International Standards Organization. *Data Communication – High Level Data Link Control Procedures – Frame Structure*, ISO 3309.

International Standards Organization. *Reference Model of Open Systems Interconnection*, ISO/TC97/SG16/N 227.

International Telecommunications Union. Data Transmission over the Telephone Network, Series V recommendations, (The Orange Book) VIII.I.

International Telecommunications Union. Series X recommendations, (The Orange Book) VIII.2.

ITT. 1985. *Revue des Télécommunications*, Vol. 59, no. 3, pp. 333–45.

Kerr, I. H., Gomberg, G. R. A., Price, W. L. and Solomonides, C. M. 1976. A simulation study of routing and flow control problems in a hierarchically connected packet switching network, *Proc. Int. Computer Communication Conference, Toronto*, August.

Leibson, S. 1983. *The Handbook of Microcomputer Interfacing*. Tab Books.

Lilen, H. 1984. *Interfaces pour microprocesseurs et micro-ordinateurs*. John Wiley.

McQuillan, J. M. 1974. Adaptive routing algorithms for distributed computer networks. Report 2831, Bolt, Beranck and Newman.

Motorola handbooks.

Rudin, H. 1976. On routing and 'delta routing': a taxonomy and performance comparison of techniques for packet-switched networks, *IEEE Trans. Communications*, COM-24, January.

Voelcker, J. 1986. Helping computers communicate, *IEEE Spectrum*, no. 3.

Wallich, P. 1985. and Zorpette, G. The innovation revolution awaits, *IEEE Spectrum*, no. 11.

Wallich, P. and Zorpette, G. 1986. Minis and mainframes, *IEEE Spectrum*, no. 1.

Glossary

Addition modulo 2 Binary addition without carry, the 'Exclusive OR' logical operation.

Aloha A network operated by the University of Hawaii using packet transmission by radio at UHF.

Alphabet A set of characters used to represent data and for which there is an agreed convention between users.

AM Amplitude modulation.

ASCII American Standard Code for Information Interchange.

Baseband The range of frequencies used by an information signal.

Baud The unit of information rate; it indicates the number of discrete states or levels which can be transmitted in one second.

Bit A contraction of binary digit; it can take the value 0 or 1.

Buffer (buffer memory) An intermediate data storage area.

Byte A group of bits used to represent a character, usually 8 bits.

Carrier A wave modulated in amplitude and/or frequency and/or phase by a signal containing information.

CCITT International Telegraph and Telephone Consultative Committee.

Channel The path along which a signal can be sent.

Circuit switching Switching similar to that used in the telephone network where communication is accomplished through a circuit established specially for this purpose and maintained between the subscribers for the duration of the communication.

Concentrator A device that receives information from several lines and sends it on a single line; it also performs the inverse operation.

Control character A character in an alphabet that is reserved for control purposes and not data transmission.

Cryptography A technique that makes the contents of a message incomprehensible to everyone except the designated destination.

Data Information expressed in a formal manner (generally digital) for processing, storage or transmission.

Datagram A packet sent in a network independently of the others and containing its own destination address.

DCE 'Data Communication Equipment' or 'Data Circuit terminating Equipment'; equipment generally provided by the telecommunication authorities and situated at the client's premises as a means of access to a circuit.

Delimiter See Flag.

Demand multiplexing A variation of time division multiplexing in which the allocation of each time slot is made as a function of the quantity of information to be transmitted.

Demultiplexer Equipment that directs data from a high-capacity or high-bandwidth channel to its appropriate destination.

DES 'Data Encryption Standard'; a standard algorithm used in cryptography for US government applications and defined in FIPS publication 46.

DTE 'Data terminal equipment'; The user's equipment that is connected to a data communication network whether specialized or not.

Duplex (Full duplex) A mode of transmission that permits communication in both directions simultaneously.

FEP 'Front end processor'; a specialized processor for communication procedure management that frees the principal computer of this task.

Flag A sequence of bits that defines the start or the end of a frame; in HDLC, 01111110.

FM Frequency modulation.

Frequency division multiplexing The combination of several analog signals on a wide bandwidth channel by modulation of carriers of different frequencies.

Full duplex See Duplex.

Half duplex Use of a circuit in one direction at a time.

Handshaking A procedure in which each signal or operation across an interface is followed by a signal or operation in the opposite direction.

HDLC 'High Level Data Link Control'; a protocol that permits users of a network to use functions at a higher level than that which corresponds simply to the transport of blocks of data.

Indicator See Flag.

Interface The boundary between two parts of a system across which interaction is completely defined.

ISO International Standards Organization.

Key A parameter used in cryptography.

Logical channel number In packet switching, several virtual calls or permanent virtual circuits can use an interface together and each is identified by this number.

Message authentification Addition of a check field to a message to monitor whether its contents have been changed in transit.

Message switching A method of operating a communication network in which messages are sent from node to node; each node must have a means of storing messages but it can start to send them before reception of the whole message.

Modem Equipment that transforms a digital signal into a signal that can be transmitted on an analog channel and converts an analog signal from a remote modem into a digital signal.

Modulation The process of changing some characteristics of a carrier wave as a function of an information signal.

Multiplexer A device that performs multiplexing.

Node A junction of two or more lines; in packet switching, a switching circuit.

Packet switching A method of operating a communication network in which messages are divided into packets that are of predetermined format and cannot exceed a certain length; these packets are transmitted from node to node (cf. Message switching).

PAD 'Packet assembler/disassembler'; a device that assembles characters into packets and the inverse operation.

Parity The property of being even or odd.

Passband The range of frequencies used by an information signal.

PM Phase modulation.

Primary station A station that directs operations at the data-link level by generating commands and interpreting the responses.

Protocol A clearly defined procedure for interaction across an interface or with a communication device.

PVC A 'permanent virtual circuit' established between two subscribers and the operator of a communication network.

Secondary station A station under the control of a primary station that sends commands to it; it interprets these and generates responses.

Simplex A circuit that can be used only in one direction.

Time division multiplexing Several channels of low throughput are sent on a channel of higher capacity by dividing access to this into separate time slots.

User authentification Verification that the user of a terminal corresponds to his claimed identity.

VC 'Virtual call'; a virtual circuit established by a subscriber at his request and cleared when communication is finished.

Virtual circuit In packet switching, a circuit that enables the sequence of packets to be conserved between two terminals.

Index